# MY LIFE IN MOTION PICTURES

## 30 Famous Movie Quotes for Day-to-Day Life

I0405582

**Written By:**

**Kelsey Mecher-Wentzloff**

Kelsey Mecher-Wentzloff

ISBN:
ISBN-13: 978-1505602173
ISBN-10: 1505602173

For my Mom and Dad.

I did it.

I love you guys with all my heart.

# CONTENTS:

Day 17: *"Come out to the coast, we'll get together, have a few laughs."* – **Die Hard (1988)**

Day 18: *"I'm just a kid from Brooklyn"* – **Captain America (2011)**

Day 19: *"You've Got Mail"* – **You've Got Mail (1998)**

Day 20: *"Are you crying? ARE YOU CRYING? There's no crying! There's NO CRYING IN BASEBALL!"* – **A League of Their Own (1992)**

Day 21: *"Even the smallest person can change the course of the future."* – **Lord of the Rings: Fellowship of the Ring (2001)**

Day 22: *"Frankly, my dear, I don't give a damn."* – **Gone with the Wind (1939)**

Day 23: *"Who's on First?"* – **The Naughty Nineties (1945)**

Day 24: *"If you don't have anything nice to say about anybody, come sit by me."* – **Steel Magnolias (1989)**

Day 25: **Casablanca (1942)**

Day 26: *"Best Day."* - **City Slickers (1991)**

Day 27: *"Boy, I got vision and the rest of the world is wearing bifocals."* – **Butch Cassidy and the Sundance Kid (1969)**

Day 28: *"Go the Distance."* – **Rocky (1976)**

Day 29: **It's a Wonderful Life (1946)**

Day 30: *"Thanks for the Memories."* – **The Big Broadcast of 1938 (1938)**

## ACKNOWLEDGMENTS:

There are so many people to acknowledge for making this book possible. First, I would like to thank my best friend, Linda, for getting me started on the NANOWRIMO challenge. If it wasn't for you Linda, I never would have even thought of writing this book.

For my Mother who told me "write what you know, and you know movies. So write something about that." Without those words I would have written something very different and these words would never have been uttered. Thanks Mom!

I would also like to express my thanks to the random citizens of America. To the lady I ran into at Meijers; to the checkout guy at FYE; to the bank tellers; the Librarians; my family and to everyone that told me their favorite quote from a movie that helped make this book possible, I thank you. You have no idea how much help you have been to me and to this book.

I would also like to thank the Writers of these Hollywood movies. You folks are the true heroes in the movie industry. Thank you for imagining the words that has transpired our lives. We owe it all to you.

# _November 1, 8:15am_

## _Day 1_

Listening to Foreigner; _Castle_ in the background; smell of coffee brewing, the smell of Vanilla Swirl candles burning; a case of Mountain Dew at the center of the futon; wearing my coffee sweat pants and my Harley Davidson pajama shirt. And both computers (my laptop and my Mac) are up and running with both Word and Works telling me it's time to fill the page. The blinking cursor is ready to move where no cursor has moved before. Yes folks. Many people would say this is one deranged child. The Gods have pity on her and many believe that they should take her out of her misery. Others would see it as a fleeting of knowledge. This is where the great masterminds used to stand, or sit, as I am currently doing. Many would say this is madness, and they would be right. A young woman who is lonely, cold, and hungry for the knowledge that is lodged inside her head is fighting to get it out. The only thing standing in her way is time; time that seems to be slipping from her grasp. Now it is November. November: the time of change. Change from falling leaves to falling snow. Change into the thinking of there is no time in the world to do what needs to be done.

Just a few months ago this young woman thought that there would be no way for her to escape the trap of time until her knight in shining armor came and rescued her from the guilt. The man who came up with *NANOWRIMO*, National November Writing Month is the knight in shining armor. I mean it. If it wasn't for him coming up with the 50,000 words in 30 days challenge, I never would have the guts to sit down and write. Just write. And he even said that I don't have to have a plot to start out; bless him. Ever since I decided to write, to become a writer, to become an inspiration to myself and to others, I have been hitting a lot of dead ends and many stories unfinished and the feeling of why should I finish them. Then my friend steered me to this pathway in life and I had to snatch it up before it took to the winds and I would have missed my opportunity to let these

memories; these fantasies go. I must. It's my destiny.
Okay that one is a little farfetched, but it's the truth.

Anyway, this man has decided my fate and I will do
everything in my power to accomplish this mission. By
tonight I have to have 1,557 words. As I am looking at
my word count, I can already see that's going to take a
while. As long as I have my coffee, and Mountain Dew I
will be just fine.

So as long as I am here I must figure out what I am
going to write about. I have thought of many things, but
nothing really sticks with me. So let's start out scratch.
It must be something that I really like to talk about. As
my mother would say "Do whatever you want to do as
long as you love doing it." As I was thinking of what my
mother said, I kept thinking about all the quotes my
mother and I share. And most of them are quotes from
movies, that we both enjoy watching.

I love watching movies. No, I mean I LOVE
watching movies. And I love quoting movies to people;
whether they are family, friends or strangers that I met
walking down the street! I could quote from movies all
day long. Some of the movies would be from now and

some would be old time movies that can be seen on Turner Classic Movies, but I would get the quote just fine and it would ALWAYS fit itself comfortably with my lifestyles. I always go back to the one thing people will understand what the heck I'm talking about: Tony DiNozzo; the character from *NCIS*. Remember him? He's the hot, good looking guy that always gets slapped in the head by Gibbs. Tony is always quoting from movies. Whatever he is doing, wherever he is at, he is quoting something from a movie that just fits with his surroundings. Ladies and Gentlemen, you just heard (or saw) my life. That's how I get through this crummy little world; by making jokes from the movies. Then I was thinking, why not make a book out of that? They do it all the time in the movies/TV shows. I could be your personal DiNozzo. Each day I will quote a famous line from a famous movie and that will be my personal quote for that day. Whatever that quote says I will try to live up to it for THAT day. 30 days 30 quotes. Pretty sweet huh? We all love quoting movies, so how about we use those quotes in our lives. It would probably improve everybody's life. So, what are WE afraid of? Yes, I said

WE. From here on out, we are all together in this. We just jumped the train; we just jumped the bridge together. We are tighter than ever and we will change our lives for the better by living with MOVIE QUOTES. So, let's get started!!

For November 1, we are going to live out our "day" with one quote from one famous movie. It's a quote that "everyone" can live by. Everybody is actually living by this quote without even realizing it. A quote from one of the greatest movies of our time. What's the quote? Which movie am I talking about? Well, ladies and germs without further ado, let's welcome the one the only opener for this day; welcome *"**Life moves pretty fast. If you don't stop and look around once in a while, you could miss it***." - Matthew Broderick from *Ferris Bueller's Day Off*. (*Applause in the background*.) I can even see him in his robe walking towards the camera quoting that. And you know what? He's right. (Of course he's right, he's Ferris Bueller don't ya know!)

Life does move pretty fast. One minute you're blowing out your first candle on your first birthday cake and then boom you're helping YOUR one year old blowing out their first birthday cake! You're going along in school finishing up your project when you wake up and you're at your high stress job finishing up a project before the board. Kids grow up too fast. They want to be so mature so fast it's sad. My dad always told me try to stay a kid as long as you can. And you know what? That's exactly what I'm going to do. I mean, yes there are many things I have to be mature in like at my job, paying for my own rent/bills that I have to pay, so I can't really keep thinking I'm just a kid, but there are so many things I really don't want to *grow out of.* Like comic books: who doesn't want to just keep reading comic books? That keeps us in the moment, and staying as a kid.

And Ferris was right; if we don't stop and look around, like smell a rose here or a daisy there, or play on the swing sets, then we are going to forget what it's all about. IT being life. IT being the world. IT being how the world can be so much fun if you stop and actually take the time to look at your surroundings.

As a librarian I am open to a lot of things. I see how the kids react to things; I see what people like too, as we librarians like to say "lose themselves into". Each book they check out is a mystery. Each story they read they relate to. That's how some of these fine people stop and look around. Many think they're losing precious time by reading a book, but that's how most people get by. That's how they sometimes "grow up" if you can. If they can see these fictional characters being the hero of the story then maybe they can to be the hero of their own story. But, I also see many of the adults come in and their just like "Blah, blah, blah, and that was my day! Yippee!" Many people don't realize that they are not just ornery, they are bored. Bored with their life. They forgot how to have fun. They forgot to laugh once in a while and actually got sucked into the vortex of the crummy world.

You see, when things go wrong in the world, people need to laugh. Whatever the joke is, whoever is giving it, people need to laugh at that joke or we are all going to go crazy. Take Bob Hope. He has seen so many things that would make a Marine cry, but he still laughed. He still cracked out jokes so that OTHERS could laugh, because he could see what the world, what the people of the world would do if they didn't just laugh at things. To me, that is stopping whatever you are doing and looking around at things that matter in life more than dollar bills or bills that need to be paid. Once you do stop whatever you are doing for like, let's say two seconds, you can actually breathe.

Do that. Take two seconds out of your busy life, sit down somewhere where you can see nature or a window that shows you the sea and take a breath. Breathe in, breathe out. See what the sea is bringing into shore, see what nature brings out to show the world what its hiding. All of that and it only takes two seconds. Then go right back to your job and you will actually see a change in the way you see things. Things will start making sense to you and you can get the work done in half the time so you can go home to your family and play monopoly: another stress level "game". Just do that. Stop; look around; and you won't miss your daughter's smile, you won't miss your son's game, you won't miss the opportunity to see your spouse grow old alongside of you and loving you even more. You'll see a huge change in the way you look at life if you just stop whatever you are doing and take a look around; smell the roses as some may put it; pay attention to the little things in life and you won't feel that you missed a dang thing in life.

Thank you, Ferris. From this quote, I believe that people will have a much better outlook of their own story. Go forth and re-watch this movie. Which quote do YOU think can help you? And how will this quote help you?

*"Life moves pretty fast. If you don't stop and look around once in a while, you could miss it."* - Matthew Broderick from *Ferris Bueller's Day Off.*

# *November 2, 10:00am*

## *Day 2*

Okay. Now that we got one quote down, 29 more to
go! Oh I can just feel the warmth of ~~hate~~, love in my
heart. I really wrote a lot in my last one. Interesting.
1,839 words just in one day! Inconceivable! Yesterday
we had the quote from *Ferris Bueller's Day Off* and I
would have to agree with some people that that quote is a
pretty good quote. And many people will understand and
can also relate to this quote. Everybody remembers that
classic film and remember many quotes from that one
movie, but that one would have to be the best one. But
for today, we are going to pick another quote that
everyone loves to say, even in that particular accent,
which just brightens almost everybody's day, (which is
interesting). Just hearing that accent, hearing this line, it
just puts a smile right on your face doesn't? I mean it
just….wait…what? I can't quite here you? What?
Which lime is it? I'm not talking about lime; I'm talking
about…..oh oh LINE?! Sorry it's kind of hard to hear

you through 1 and 0 (binary code for you computer illiterates). Which line am I talking about? Oh, I'm sorry. I didn't give it? As we say in my generation: "My Bad!" Okay the quote for today is the one we all cherish: ***"Mama always said life was like a box of chocolates. You never know what you're gonna get."*** – Tom Hanks in *Forrest Gump*. Oh, yea. You all knew that one was coming.

Come on, let's face it. You're walking down the street; you see a little boy asking his mother why life isn't fair, and she says to him very quietly hoping no one will see saying "Life is like a box of chocolates, son. You never know what you're gonna get." I just cherish that moment. Because I can see Sally Field looking up to her son, Tom Hanks, saying Life is like a box of chocolates…..not realizing that that line will be used for generations and generations. It's such an inspiration to us all really.

In life, you never really know what you're going to get. A good day, meeting nice people, not getting run over on your way to work, choices are being made correctly, those doors are all opening and people are giving you things… (Okay Kelsey they get it.) Then we will never know if that day is actually going to be a bad day, meeting mean people that do you wrong, actually getting run over on your way to work, choices turning out badly maybe even costing you your job, and those doors that were supposed to stay open just smack ya where the good Lord split ya! Just remember this quote: *Life is like a box of chocolates. You never know what you're gonna get.* Think about that for just a sec. You have a box of chocolates in your lap. You open it up, pick one piece and think, I wonder if it is going to be caramel, or or maybe it's got nuts in it. You never know what you are gonna get, and it's your decision to just wing it and choose one or put the candy back in the box and never open it again.

There are two kinds of people in this world: those that are willing to try anything and those that don't or won't (however you see it). Those that try anything mostly will open up the box and try any kind of chocolate, no matter what kind it really is; they will try it and live with it. Then there are the kind of people that will take one look at it, and wait till someone comes by and TELLS them which one it is, which one they can eat. They can't just TRY it; they won't venture into making their own choice of what they want.

Without making choices what else are we supposed to do? How else are we supposed to grow? With someone telling us what kind of candy is in which container, we will never understand the need to explore; trying new things. Take things as they are, learning from it and moving on. Learning from taking whatever chocolate comes at you, helps you later on in life. It helps us to anticipate. It helps us to be observant of our surroundings. It helps you to see things from a different perspective. Don't just go with seeing, but also go with what feels right. What you feel helps you move on in this world. Just seeing what things are and not questioning it, is just dumb. You could get hurt by doing things like that. How will you be able to find someone in your life if you don't take chances? Taking chances is what life is all about, and if you don't learn from those choices, then you won't be able to move on with your life. You'll just be stuck in that rot, and you won't be able to move forward in time. So take a chance. Just pick a chocolate and move on. Let your fingers go over the box of chocolates and pick one. Once you pick one, you will see where it will take you, what you can learn from it, and then go back to that box and move on to the next thing in life.

It's an interesting way of looking at life, if you actually look at it. Being adventurous has actually saved our race, but then we turn right around and say that it's not good for the soul, and it's a sin to go out and do things that are not of the "order". Not really knowing what that meant when I was little, I'll put it into more laymen's terms: following your own dreams and not following someone else's. You are making your own choices and living with the praises or the consequences of those choices. And that is how our race has gotten so far in life. By making those tough choices, by opening that can of worms and letting everything out we have actually progressed in life.

How can I use this quote in my life? How can I see what Forrest Gump saw when he was remembering what his momma said about that box of chocolates? I guess what I can say for certain is that I'm not going too…..wait.  It needs to be…..I SHOULD not hesitate to open that box of chocolates.  Before I open it, I should realize and understand that I won't be able to distinguish which kind of chocolate is which, but I should be able to open it up with ease and be ready to dive in and "go with the flow" of eating whichever one that comes up.  I think by not knowing what I will pick I think that's what makes our lives a whole lot better to live in because if we knew what the next scene was before it's even played, we wouldn't want to watch the movie.  It would get very boring and it wouldn't be very educational.  Go forth and re-watch this movie.  Which quote do YOU think can help you?  And how will this quote help you?

*"Mama always said life was like a box of chocolates.  You never know what you're gonna get."* – Tom Hanks in *Forrest Gump*.

# *November 3, 9:00am*

## *Day 3*

Well, here we are again. Day 3. And actually I'm waking up in the morning all jazzed about writing. I'm so pumped about this; I can't believe that my fingers are catching every single word that is popping inside my head. It's so….man, my fingers are going to hurt by tonight, I can tell you that! That's okay. I guess that's the price I have to pay, right?

At least I'm actually doing something about it. I'm actually not even sure if this sequence of quotes is going to be the EXACT sequences I will be using for the final book, but this is what it's going to be for right now. Okay….here is your third (if it's going to be that) quote for today. And it's actually a fun quote. You wouldn't think it would be very memorable but it has its qualities. Something in the way this character/actor said it in the right sequence of events just made it stand out more than all the other quotes that were used in this particular movie.

It's from one of the greatest movies, the words came from one of the greatest actors of all time; well, I believe all the LADIES will all agree with me here. The quote is:

Elizabeth Swan: *"One of these days you're going to have the chance to do something right!"*

Captain Jack Sparrow: *"Oh, I love those moments, I like to wave at them as they pass by!"*

It's from the movie *Pirates of the Caribbean: Dead Man's Chest.* Who doesn't like Pirate movies? *Arrgh me mates!!!* One of the best lines ever written I supposed (if you're into that sort of thing). Now you must be wondering what sort of memorable quote such as that should be doing in such a book as this? How can this quote, for one day, change my outlook on life itself? Jack Sparrow, I mean, CAPTAIN Jack Sparrow was a thief, a Pirate, and a bad one at that. He wouldn't help anyone but himself, (of course he ends up saving everybody else in the end) and he always takes the rotten way out (meaning that old long line of Pirate traditions of fighting to run away).  At the time of this quote, he was trying to get away by leaving his friends behind, and he wouldn't take no for an answer.  Elizabeth Bennett was trying to make him change his course, and also change his ways.  Captain Jack wouldn't hear of it.  He knows what the right choice was, he knew what he was about to do was the wrong one, but he's like "Who cares?  I don't always have to make the right choice. The right choice only gets me and MY SHIP killed."  Yes, it is very funny the way he said it, and I know all of you that are reading this are remembering that scene and how Johnny Depp does it, you are probably laughing right now.  I know I was, and how funny it was.  But answer me this, do you ever feel that way sometimes?  Whenever an opportunity starts knocking on your door, you either say come right on in or wave at them as you go out?  Are you Elizabeth or are you Jack?  (Sorry Sparrow…) I mean, Captain Jack?  Are you one of those that instead of doing the right choice in something, you just run away from it?  This should turn out to be one interesting day.

"The chance to do something right."  What does that even mean?  Do something right?  Is it more like do something kind for someone? Or like making the right choice in whatever situation arises. More so the latter.

It makes sense to me that Elizabeth is trying to tell Captain Jack that there will be a moment in your life where you are going to have to choose the right path that will save not only yourself but everyone around you and not have to be so selfish in doing so. But Captain Jack will hear none of it. If he makes the right choice in whatever happens, then he is a humble man, he is a righteous man, not a Pirate! A Pirate lives by no rules. A Pirate steals to make HIMSELF righteous, to make himself rich. Anybody else tries to meddle with that, take him out.

That really leaves out the chance of making the right choices in life now don't? So now, I guess we must ask ourselves, what are we? The kind of human beings that will let the right choices make our lives, take over and let us be righteous; or are we the kind of human beings that will wave goodbye to the right and just live in the moment and let our selfish ways be the best of us? No I didn't think so. Even if we don't mean too, we usually want the best for ourselves, but we also don't want to hurt anybody else. We have this "feeling" I guess you could say, that when pushed into a situation like that, we want to protect, we want to save and we want to make the right choice knowing that the wrong choice will only endanger ourselves and our friends.

We can also look at this quote from the point of jobs; families; and the way we make a living. The right choice: we find a good job, the one that pays well for our families, making sure that our families are well fed and there are clothes on their backs: too, the way we make a living, are we living on the streets or do we have a roof over our heads protecting us from the rain? The wrong choice: get a crappy job or no job at all just living off the (broken) government: families are starving because you are at a strip club gambling away the mortgage money: the broken down homes, choices that actually lead you to living at the bottom of a bridge. Are you going to "wave goodbye as they go by" to play poker with your families mortgage money? Or are you the kind that will say, no, no poker for me today, I must pay my mortgage and then the rest will be for the food on the table. It is so sad to see in this day and age that there are so many people that will just wave bye bye to their right choices and stick with the wrong ones, not even caring what happens to the people around them.

This quote, this message is a little short one, mostly because it just seems so simple:  Choose the right choice if you want to live right.  Wave goodbye to your future and suffer the consequences.  Easy, right?  Well, then why do we have so many Captain Jack's living under bridges?  Why are there so many welfare people?  Because just like Captain Jack, they got so used to living like that, they don't ever want to turn back to being right!  They like the idea of people handing them things…not being responsible for things anymore when someone else is fitting the bill…kicking back and doing nothing but "wave bye bye".

Now my question for you is how do we change Captain Jack?  How did Elizabeth get Captain Jack to turn around and help his fellow crew mates?  Now I could tell you how she did it, but then it would be like handing you the answers to the final test; handing you things like we mentioned before.  This one you're going to have find the answer for yourselves.

Mostly because the answer is actually different for everybody.  Everybody has a different outlook on life and if I just give you the answer right now, then you're going to think that this applies to you too when in fact, you could have another approach to this that actually fits your lifestyle which maybe different than mine.

Good luck finding it.  And please, stop waving goodbye to the right choices in your life and start opening that door and say "Hi, how are ya?"  Try it….you could surprise yourself, like Captain Jack Sparrow was in the end.  Go forth and re-watch this movie.  Which quote do YOU think can help you?  And how will this quote help you?

~ Keira Knightley:  *"One of these days you're going to have the chance to do something right!"*

 Johnny Depp:  *"Oh, I love those moments, I like to wave at them as they pass by."*

- *Pirates of the Caribbean:  Dead Mans Chest*

# *November 4, 12:00pm*

## *Day 4*

There is nothing better than spending the day with your mother. I think if we spend at least a good half hour with anyone of our family members, more importantly your mother, I think we would all learn something about them and about ourselves. My mother is very much into quilting. She has projects that involve quilts, and then she has quilts. She is so fascinated by fabrics that seeing her without a quilt in her hands seems out of place. She would be up in her Studio sewing away on a project that she or someone she knows hasn't finished yet which are called UFO's (Unfinished Objects) and I'm back at the house starving like heck trying to find something to eat! It is so tragic! (As you can see I'm very melodramatic.)

Well, she also likes to go to these Arts and Crafts shows that occur every year and try to sell a lot of her fabulous work. There are so many of the same projects for sale, all the same stuff and the same prices for them all. There are some that have crafts that were handcrafted. Like some blankets, some of the jewelry are handmade; then you go down the hallway and there are a few people that have the same blankets the same type of jewelry and it's from the factory (stores that they work for) and they're selling them for much more than the crafters are and getting more and more people going to them and buying their stuff than the people that actually worked hard making them!

There are also the same people that come: the kind that just look, comment, about nice things that were made but don't buy anything; the kind that likes it and buys it without even thinking twice about the price and it has the same Dutch people year after year. Like they say, "If ya ain't Dutch, then ya ain't much", and they are so tight about their money. They love to look at all the projects but they just don't like to buy any of them. Thinking they should at least get some kind of discount just because they live around the craft show. Then they take a look at their crafts get the measurements and then go home to make their own then come back to another craft show and sell theirs! Gotta love them! (Sarcastic there)

But, my mother loves going to these shows. She see's friends, she hangs out with her girlfriends, and gets to show off what she's done. She has glaucoma which is a disease in her eyes, and it sort of blinded her and she can't drive herself anywhere. We joke and say that I'm her seeing-eye child. We live in such a rural area and they won't allow her to have a seeing-eye dog so I filled that position for her.

So there is a reason why I'm here, but I'm also here to support my mother. She loves it; she loves meeting new people and seeing what they like so then she can improve on her quilts to what people out in the world actually would like to buy and that's enough for me. Yes, I have to agree, it gets a little boring, people looking at you are telling the same story of how each quilt was made, and they are like "OH MY GOSH THAT IS LIKE SO AMAZING!! I CAN'T BELIEVE YOU MADE THAT?!" Then they just like walk away like they forgot why they came over to our table.

It gets old very fast. Sometimes I just start making stuff up so they would stay around and maybe by chance they would like just buy something. But, this is for my

Mother. She loves these types of people, (Sarcastic again. Man, I'm all over this) these types of meetings and she gets to show off her projects. It's always fun to see her light up when someone comments on her projects.

This pretty much has nothing to do with the quote I'm going to write about but I need to have 50,000 words for the end of the month. But I guess this story does go somewhere close to what the quote is. You see my mother's place to go is her studio. That's her place of Zen; her place to get away from the crummy world and live in Peace and Harmony; no more worrying about anything, no telling people what to do and not having to worry about when the bills come and when they are due. As others would say, she is hiding inside her shell; she's got her own personal bubble that she hides into.

I like to say that that is her Never Never Land. A place where she can hide from the world but still have fun doing things. I love calling it her Never Never Land. The place where she can do anything; the place where she can be anything; a place where no one gets older, you stay a kid all the time and you never have to plan your life ever again. Whatever you want to do, you do. You want to have fun, you will have fun. So my next quote for you all is: *"**So come with me, where dreams are born, and time is never planned. Just think of happy things, and your heart will fly on wings, forever, in Never Never Land!**"* –from *Peter Pan*.

This was always an interesting line for me to think about because people literally really wish that there was a place called Never Never Land. They want to believe that there is a place where people don't grow up, where people don't have responsibilities to go home to and they can always think of happy things and can actually fly through the clouds. That their dreams will always come true whatever those dreams are.

I always wondered why? Why dream of such a place? You will never grow, you will never mature, you will never proceed into your destiny, you will never have the responsibility, the respect that you most definitely need. Why do some people just pretend that there is such a thing as a place other than now? Why not live in the moment? Why live in a fantasy?

Because the real world SUCKS!!! It's a horrible crummy world out there and people just lost respect for everybody else. Nobody cares about their neighbors anymore; nobody cares about helping their friends when they are low but they care about only one person and one thing in their lives: Themselves and their money!!! That's all they will ever care about now. Their money and if they lose their money they lose their sanity. They lose their sanity; they lose who they really are inside.

So, they pretend, they have fantasies that there is a world out there where nobody is going to ask you for your mortgage, for your money and you will never have to be responsible for anything else. How much fun would that be? Be the center of your own universe and there is a universe out there that will allow you to do that. When kids grow up to be grownups they forget what their world is all about. They grow up too quick, and then they try so hard to get back to being a kid. So, why? Why do we have to grow up so quick? Just remember this quote and you will spend a few minutes just pretending. Just fantasies about something that will take them away from the hardships of their lives and just think about happy things and fly away from their troubles!

That's sometimes how I feel whenever I'm working at the library. I feel like Peter Pan, and Neverland is the library, the little island that is at the second star to the right and straight on till morning! All those books around me, all those little adventures that have been explored or waiting to be explored. Every time a young person opens a book and jumps for joy over the new adventure they are about to partake, in my eyes, a fairy is born.

Now this is to say that I would have to believe in such things and if there is ever a fairy in need I would definitely clap my hands as loud as I can to make sure that that fairy will live. And when that child is done reading that book, the fairy will still live on for the adventure will stay with that child forever and ever and will be passed down generation to generation. It will grow, it will manifest into a great being that you could not imagine.

As I said before, my mother's studio is HER Neverland. For my father it would have to be his workshop. He works on Appliances: stoves, microwaves, dishwashers, washing machines and dryers. He also works on lawnmowers, snow blowers. So he is always out in his workshop working on somebody's lawnmower that won't start or he'll be tearing up a dishwasher and putting it back together just because he can! That's his Neverland.

For me, it's my library like I said. Everybody has a Neverland in their life; it's just finding it is kind of hard. For some it may seem to be many different places but if you look really really hard into finding that second star to the right I believe you will find it. It's just kind of hard to find through all this smog, (lies, betrayals, debts to be paid, is the kind of smog I was referring too) but you will be able to find it if you just give enough effort to look for it.

Think of your place. Where do you think it is that your dreams will be born, will they will be able to take flight and not worrying about money or the time that will be spent? But the real question is: Will you go? Go forth and re-watch this movie. Which quote do YOU think can help you? And how will this quote help you?

*"So come with me, where dreams are born, and time is never planned.  Just think of happy tings, and your heart will fly on wings, forever, in NEVER NEVER LAND!"* – Peter Pan

# *November 5, 8:05am*

## *Day 5*

Ladies and gentlemen, this next quote is something that doesn't even need introduction. This quote you could actually just state it, and there it is, you don't need any explanation about the quote, it's actually very self-explanatory by itself. Ever since this quote came out in movies, everybody has used it. Whatever the troubles are in life, people that understand this quote uses it to strengthen their spirits.

The quote for November 5 is for all the geeks out there that are like me, that cherish this quote and apply this quote to their lives. The quote for today is: *"**Do, or do not. There is no try**."* –Yoda, from *Star Wars: The Empire Strikes Back*. Yes, yes. I know. *STAR WARS*! What is it with geeks and their *Star Wars*? But if you actually pay attention to all the little details and the sayings and all the aliens and…well you get the picture, you will see a lot of things that you can use for your life.

A lot of quotes are used in those movies that you can use in making your life better, but this one just oversees all the other quotes. Even *"May the Force Be with You"* quote! Of course, it's just my opinion, but if you really look into the quote and THEN your life, you will see how you can use Yoda's quote to make your life even better.

Having trouble making your quota? Having trouble thinking you're not good enough for the job? Thinking the boss made a mistake picking you for making the project to present it to the board? Trying so hard to please everybody else that it just makes you stress even more, and then nothing gets done? Then you need to wake up from your slumber, smack yourself on the back of the head (I like to call them the Gibbs Slap) and rent or you should have gotten your own by now, rent *Star Wars: The Empire Strikes Back* and pay attention to Yoda. Yoda is trying to teach Luke Skywalker that size does not matter when you are using the Force, and stop TRYING to accomplish things. You actually DO finish it, or you DON'T. It's that easy.

You must have the effort to finish things, but you also have to have the mind set to actually do it. Nobody is going to DO it *for* you. You must DO it; you must finish it to actually feel that accomplishment. I read somewhere on the internet that actually fits in with this quote: "A teacher of mine once made the point by asking me to "try to get out of that chair" that I was sitting in. When I stood up, she said, "No, I asked you to **TRY** to get out of the chair, not to actually get out of it." I hesitated for a few minutes, sitting and then almost starting to get up and then sitting again. "See?" she said. "*Trying* is not *doing*. If you're going to do something, then do it...""" Very interesting isn't it? "There is no try" means that one should not approach a task with the attitude that only an attempt will be made. Instead when approaching a task the mentality should be to either accomplish it or not. What he's trying to say is that you either do something or don't, you don't just try.

Try is a useless word. It doesn't mean anything. To try is to attempt, but you can't really try and do anything. There are only actions you have taken and actions you haven't taken. You can aim at a goal, take various actions and fail to reach the goal. You can even attempt actions outside of your capability, but in the end, you end up with results based upon actions you can perform. I think by saying that you'll give it a "try", you invite uncertainty. Either you succeed or you fail. There's no middle ground, so don't think like there is one. If you "try" and fail, it creates the sense that you didn't go at it with full cylinders. (Put a little car reference there for my men) But if you "do not", at least you attempted it with all of your strength.

"Going to try" is even worse. When? How? Why? Are you going to succeed or are you going to fail? There is no defiant meaning behind that saying "going to try", so why bother? It's all about beliefs as well. When you're really committed you think "I'm gonna do this" not "I'm gonna try to do this"... You put yourself in a mindset that makes you think it's more possible, or should I say it becomes more possible because you have that mindset. The reason why people say they tried is because it looks good; you made an attempt, even though you still didn't get the results. But in the end, it's not the attempt you want; it's the results of successful actions. That's what stops most people, they stop at the trying, not at the success.

There's really nothing else I could stress for this quote. If you are familiar with the movie, great, you know what I'm talking about. If you have not seen the movie, then you need a Gibbs Slap very quickly and watch the movie. If not a fan for sci-fi, then just watch it to see this quote in action. Don't try, you will fail. Do it, or don't. So what are you? A Doer or a Do Not? That is the question. Go forth and re-watch this movie. Which quote do YOU think can help you? And how will this quote help you?

*"Do, or do not. There is no try."* – Yoda, from *Star Wars: The Empire Strikes Back*

# *November 6, 9:15pm*

## *Day 6*

Watching *Star Wars: The Revenge of the Sith*. A very good movie; not as good as the older ones, but it's still a good one. Amazing how he believed so much in the Sith Lord that he could have so much power to protect his wife that it was used against him. So much love, so much emotion that can corrupt your thinking; your logic is thrown out the window because of love.

Because of that want of power; the power to do almost anything you want has such great consequences. And in that movie it was because of love. Love corrupted him so much that he thought he could possess that much power and not have consequences for his actions. It makes you think doesn't? Do I really want all that power? The responsibility of my actions because of an amazing power? Is it really that important to have such great power just to protect the ones that you love even if that means you must suffer for the rest of your life?

Interesting enough, humans have shown that yes, it is important. That one moment, that one decision it is important to them to have that control over others for their love. We have not yet learned to process what it would mean, what it would become if we possess that power and what it would mean for the rest of the world. Not realizing it could kill others and even the ones that you love if you just jump in and take over. Sad thing is there is no turning back. As the Doctor would say, the world would collapse and the Paradox would come and kill. (For those that are deprived of watching anything great, that was from the BBC show *Doctor Who*. I feel for you that don't know who he is. Wait, no, not feel. Sorrow. That's the feeling. Sadness. (LOL)). This actually reminds me of a great quote I heard once from the movie *Spider Man*. Of course I have heard this quote from other movies, I think it was used by Bettie Davis in *All About Eve* but then of course I have to remember who I'm talking to. My generation. A generation that is deprived of watching and understanding old movies. So sad. Anyway, you will understand this quote if I use it from *Spider Man*: "***With great power comes great responsibility.***" –Toby Maguire from *Spider Man*. A great movie, if you like comics and that sort of thing. Parker went through a lot to come to that realization of what power would mean to one. For now that he possess the gift of the "macho spider" he will have to face things that he has never faced before; things that are now in his control and if used right he would do good; used for wrong intentions, could result in people dying or love ones turned against each other. He has those responsibilities to do greatness, if he uses his power for good, and not just for HIS intentions but the intentions of everyone else. If not used properly, he will corrupt into evil and never will be able to change the things he has done.

Now this is an interesting thought, how can I use this quote to change my days in life? Easy; capture a radioactive spider, make it bite me and I turn into *Spider Man*; or catch a meteorite from Krypton and get powers that is beyond belief......okay, okay. Back to reality here. Call the *Doctor* and fly around in *TARDIS* and set new rules to the new…Okay okay I'm stopping now.

Someone once said that I am the Lady of my own story. Whatever my life is to become it's MY decision and no else's. I must decide how I am going to live my life out and which decisions are going to be good not just to me, but to the people that are around me. I have great power. The power of my life and the lives of the people around me. I have such huge responsibilities for MY actions that could affect the decisions of the people around me. (No pressure) but that is how it is for everyone else. Whatever you decide, it could affect the lives of everyone around you. So, it is true. ***With great power come great responsibility*** is not just something for heroes that have imaginary power, or gifts that no other human could possess but it is also for us puny humans that have something much greater than those fancy powers.

We have a heart, we have a soul and we are also Human. We say that not realizing how much that means. We humans have the ability to adapt to things that are around us; we have learned so much about our past that we try to move on and not make the same mistakes again. We learn from our mistakes and we try to overcome them by trying something else. Doing more than is called upon us, is how we survive.

That is another thing that we differ from any other race (if there are any), we learn how to survive. We try everything we can, which is learning. We learn very quickly how to survive or how to die. We still have a long way to go before we can call ourselves fit, but we have also learned that when one has power, that one person has the opportunity to do well for the world, or they will corrupt that power to gain their own advantage and their choices can put terror into the minds of others.

With the knowledge that such power can be obtained, could really not just devastate the world, but it will also devastate the person itself.....Go forth and re-watch this movie. Which quote do YOU think can help you? And how will this quote help you?

*"With great power comes great responsibility."* - Toby Maguire-*Spider Man*

# *November 7, 5:41pm*

## *Day 7*

People.  Citizens.  Readers from the Planet called Earth.  Welcome to another day of meditating on Quotes from Famous Movies program.  I am honored with your presence once again on this grateful day!  For this is another day of contemplating; of looking at one's self and deciding on what he/she must do to make their Hue stronger over time.  For once your Hue is restored to perfection, and then we as a group will get together and sing, drink coffee and dance in the rain and, and, AND TAKE OVER THE WORLD!!!

### MUAHHHAHHHAH!

Sorry, I had to do something different in the beginning of my quotes and that was the best I could do!! (I thought it was funny.)  In other news, we are in a new day, so that has got to mean a new quote for all you suckers out there that actually are reading this book.  (If you just picked this book off the shelf, and just happened to flip to this day, I'm not all that crazy. Just finished watching *Dr. Horrible's Sing-Along Blog*, so I guess I am a little crazy. But go ahead and buy this book, IT'S GREAT!!!) As you can see I am a very coffee deprived girl and I haven't had any cups today. For some odd reason, I have no money in my pocket right now to get coffee SOI'MSTARTINGONMYWITHDRAWALSYMPTOM S of having no coffee! Oh yea, this day is going to be a great day.

But this next quote is an awesome quote. I love this quote. Everything about this quote and what this quote stands for is everything I need. I was actually stumped on a quote for today. I couldn't quite pick a quote for this audacious day. Since today is the day that I do not have coffee I will need to ramble on about something, and why not about a great quote like this one. To be completely honest, I actually did not pick this quote out. I had the idea of the movie, but a quote from this particular movie I could not do. So I called the one person that could give me a quote to work on; one person who has loved this movie ever since it came out; the one person who actually surrounds his life with this one movie. And the lucky person is: My Big Brother.

CRASH!! BAM!!! BANG!!! Think of any comic strip with those words on it, then you will know what I just did at that moment. Let me take a moment and tell you all a little bit about my brother. I already talked about my mother, so now it's my brother's turn to turn all bashful and embarrassed! My brother is about 17 years older than I am, and he's better looking than me, and he's just a tad bit taller than I.

He had a tough childhood; trying to grow up too fast to help his mother out during some tough times; trying to get along with kids at school which is like a German soldier having tea with an American soldier while killing each other. My brother learned how to take care of others while forgetting how to take care of himself. He learned how to move with the changes in life. He knows the differences between making the right choices, knowing the differences between good and evil and he knows how to help others learn the right doings and the wrong doings in life.

He reads philosophers and shares them with anybody who will bend their ear. He loves C.S. Lewis, M. Scott Peck and many more great authors of our time. He also understands what you need to do in this world to get ahead of the times, and he also knows that having money will help you live a comfy life but also not letting it run your life and become the only thing to strive for.

And my brother loves to take care of me. When I was little, I used to get letter after letter: How are ya? How's school? "Remember Princess Kels, school is very important for whatever you want to get into. You want to get into something that will be fun and something that you like to do, but it also has to be able to fund your life. You better be making enough money to support yourself but also be doing something that you love." My brother found out that he is a very good salesperson, so that's what he does. He deals with million dollar companies like for example NASA. He's sort of like a…. I believe it's safe to say that he's not hurting for money. But, he had to work very hard to get where he is now; he didn't have family money that dropped out of thin air and was *given* to him. No, no. He *ACTUALLY* had to find a job himself and he had to work hard for it. Shocking I know. Sometimes three jobs at a time to support himself, and yes he complained like everybody else, but he knows now what it takes to be happy, and live without feeling like you're forgetting to pay your bills on time.

Everybody wonders how rich people get their money and how can they get it, too? Follow my brother's steps. Take care of yourself first; find a good job that will give you food on the table and a roof over your head; then think about maybe getting a job that will pay big bucks. Don't be looking for that job just yet, you are still prime at the age of 40; don't try to work too hard at finding a big money suspense job at the age of 20. Work odd jobs around, get those credits building on your name and before you know it, you will be able to support yourself, your family and have a nice roof over your head. Anyways, that's what he taught me and that's what he keeps telling me for the past 20 years. He even has books for me to read: *The Road Less Traveled* by M. Scott Peck; *Rich Dad Poor Dad* by Robert Kiyosaki. It worked out great for him, so why not me?

There are so many questions that I have always asked him about life and how do you get through certain things, but because my life has mostly been all about movies, I asked him one day what was his favorite movie. He said there is "only one movie that really spoke to me. A movie that gets me every time I see it. One movie that can explain what I have been going through and it also answers many of my own questions that I have about life and work."

So I asked him the same question that you are asking me right now. I asked him what movie is that. I'm no dunce. I know that if this movie helped HIM maybe it could help me. I believe you folks already know which movie I'm talking about. It's a wonderful (should be called) classic movie of all time. The *National Lampoon's Christmas Vacation*! Gotcha!! LOL! That was funny. Na, the movie that I was talking about is none other than *Jerry Maguire* with Tom Cruise and Cuba Gooding Jr. You really believe in all the conversations Tom Cruise has with himself, or with Cuba Gooding Jr. I even asked my brother what is his favorite quote from that movie. He said that he has a lot of favorite quotes that he likes to quote to other people, but a quote for himself; he said that there is only two. **"*I hated myself, Na Na here is what was, I hated my place in the world*"** and also "*Ambassador of Quan*." I really like the first one because it really makes you rethink yourself. I like to use the metaphor, Man in the Mirror, saying every time you look at yourself in the mirror what do you see? But I believe that more people are more familiar with the "*Ambassador of Quan*." So there it is folks. My new quote for today: "*Ambassador of Quan*," by Cuba Gooding Jr. through the movie *Jerry Maguire*.

Now just to clear the air, Cuba Gooding Jr. was not talking about Quan as a country or a state. No he was talking about realizing that you need others to not only succeed but to travel in any kind of journey. If you look up what Quan is in the Urban-Dictionary, it means "when you are one with something." Now what does that really mean? How can you be one with something? It means that you are complete with something. Like a husband. He is "complete" with his wife. He is whole with her. You know how writers will have it that if you lose your spouse it's like a chunk of your heart is missing, because your "other half" is gone. That's what "being one with something" means to me. Once you find that something, you will be one, you will be whole. You will be able to, let's say conquer the world. You are stronger with that one, you are a better person because of that one and you will have the knowledge and the respect for that one.

Many people out there in the world that have finally found that "one", their "Quan" they get all stuck up about it. It's like they found it, nobody else will and nobody can do what they can do. They become like snobs walking around Earth talking down to us "normal" people. And then they think that they are capable of doing anything to anyone and will actually do it without thinking of the consequences. If it fits into their schedule, then that's it. It doesn't matter to them that other people have lives and families that they need to look out for. Whatever that will profit the snobs is good enough for them! So as to you people that are reading this book (and God Bless you for doing that by the way!) have a few choices when you have found your "one" or one "Quan". Would you sulk up to others and say, "oh yea…I've got my Quan, I'm the Ambassador of Quan, aren't you?" Or are you like "I'M THE AMBASSADOR OF QUAN!!! Let's just keep that between you and me, hey?" When you are finding your Quan you are combining your special skills that no one else has. No one in this universe has the same type of skill that you have (unless you meet your better half when you get into a magnetic storm and meet your universal self (Star Trek)) and you combine that skill with love and respect. Something no one else can offer to you but yourself! Having that respect for oneself actually is the Quan. You have mastered at something; you need the respect of what you have done and the only person that can do that but also love you for what you have done is yourself!! You must take care of yourself, before you can move on towards others. Then once you can help yourself, and you move on to helping others then that is where you will find your Quan. You will find that you are indeed the *Ambassador of Quan*, and that you CAN do most anything with the help of whatever makes you whole! For me: I would have to say my writing is my Quan. In the *Jerry Maguire* movie Cuba Gooding Jr. was talking about being the ultimate football player which he combined with the love and respect from his wife and from his manager, Jerry Maguire. I get that about writing, and I get the love and respect from you folks that are reading this right now. I am the Ambassador of Quan, and I will rule the writing universe!! Step aside James Patterson…there's a new kid in town!!! Go forth and re-watch this movie. Which quote do YOU think can help you? And how will this quote help you?

*"**Ambassador of Quan**"* - Tom Cruise from *Jerry Maguire*

# *November 8, 10:38am*

## *Day 8*

Love.  Love is patient, love is kind.  Love is Roses are red, Violets are blue.  Love can be almost anything you want it to be.  Love is in the air, love is in the trees. Every time you look up in the air, love is there too.  Love can also hurt you.  Love can destroy you.  Love can destroy the people in your life, and without you looking, it can destroy your world.  Love can kill you.  Without you even realizing it, you are love's bitch.

Right now it is 10:38 in the morning.  I'm wearing my "writing" clothes.  Drinking coffee to charge those neurons in my brain, and listening to *Foreigner*.  Again. I don't know why, but their music just soothes me.  It helps me to write and it like clears my mind of anything but writing and the song.  Mostly I listen to "*I Wanna Know What Love Is*"; fitting for that is the topic for today.  I know, I know.  I should wait till Valentine's Day to bring this up, but the contest only allows

November for right now, so I'm writing about it right now. And of course, love is a subject for every day. Every day we mess with love and love messes with us 24/7, even if we want to stop. Once we set our course on love, we just want to know more about it, want to know how love feels.

Love. It is an interesting subject; it's an interesting lesson to be learned. Without love, we wouldn't really function that well. We would be looking at life in black and white and miss all that grey and color area. Everything is so simple, everything is so content. Love; well, actually love jumbles that all up. It makes you see in color, it makes your world twist all around. You'd be thinking up was down and down was up. Many psychiatrists, many anthropologists and writers have tried to piece love together. How it works, how we must "overcome" it sometimes, and how to control it. Psychiatrists try to show you that it is mostly all in the mind and the mind can be controlled. (Vulcan's in my book). Anthropologists get inside what our ancestors did and try to change for the greater good. They don't really "help" perse but, they do try to understand it all. Not very clearly, and sometimes wrong. But the only ones out of that whole bunch that actually understand about Love and understand that you really can't control ones love are the writers. Either they are the writers of stories, or the writers of songs that are to be sung, it is the writers that really understand the meaning behind the word Love.

Many people believe that the only way that they will understand Love and be able to GET love is through Sex. Yes, yes, I know. I said the four letter word. (Sex, sex, sex the boys are marching!!!) But right now it is necessary to say it. Many writers of songs try to tell you (through the song) that Love is something deeper than having Sex. Having sex is a plus in love. No, no. Love is more than sex. Sex is just something to have for those few minutes (or however long you can sustain being in that form (my goodness gracious I'm turning into; not good, MAYDAY!!!!)) Love is something that you will have for years and years. It will always be inside your heart; it will always warm you and will never leave you. Yes, I understand, that there are LOTS of songs that are about heartbreaks, but you will still have that love inside you, or you wouldn't have heartbreak.

Actually having a heartbreak proves to you that you can love. It also actually defines you. It defines who and what kind of person you are. For you still love the one that left, and it hurts. That feeling ladies and gentlemen, is just another definition of Love.

Then there is another kind of love; a love that we still don't understand why we venture in the area, but it's always there. That sense of love for one, but the other isn't quite sure. There is pleasure; there is the sense of if not being too close to the other you will feel like dying. The love that makes one crazy for the other and the other, how do we humans put it? Hard to get? For some reason, we women have decided to play that game. The game of hard to get; the game of you must come after me, you must fight for me, you must defend my honor before I will surrender to you and say "I Love You".

Interesting enough, the men like to play along and will chase as long as it takes for you to surrender your love to them. You must be wondering why I'm talking about this tough subject, and a subject that I am unfamiliar with at that. You see, I have never been in love; well, loves like that: between a man and a woman.

I love my parents, I love my family, but I have not yet had the chance to love a man the way I am talking here. I never had a boyfriend during school, for in my eyes, the boys around me just have not grown up yet. And I had school work to worry about, not if my shirt will impress my boyfriend. I was too young to even consider anything like that.

But how do I know what it would feel like? How would I know what to do in a situation of boyfriend and girlfriend, stuff? How do I know so much? How can I HELP you in this field when I have yet to have the experience myself? You see, even in High School I used to help my fellow classmates with this problem. If they were arguing with their boyfriends or even their girlfriends, for I helped the guys out too, they would feel the urge to talk about it with me, and somehow I helped them. I won't go into details but it's like I'm their counselor on love and the way I do it is that they must find their own way to the answer to their problems. They started to get smart about dating but then they also started getting smart on the fact that I haven't dated, nor have I a boyfriend. How is that I know so much, they would ask?

Simple. I watch movies. I listen closely to the words in the love songs. I read many many books that portray this type of subject many times, and I have realized one thing that helped me in life: Love is a dangerous thing. If not grasped correctly it could destroy you and your lover. So I understand before I jump into anything. I'm not saying that I'm going to have the perfect relationship because I "understand" but the mere fact that I do understand and I will work harder for the relationship then just some crush.

I know what it meant for Bogart to let Bergman on that plane with another man. I know what it meant for Mr. Darcy. How Jane Austin can write such dreary books for the ladies on this subject. And my favorite movie (well, it was my Mother's favorite, and she always dragged me into watching it so NOW it is my favorite movie) to watch the examples of how Love can either destroy you in the end, or conquer over all is a movie that I believe we should all have watched before we even decide to have a boyfriend, or a girlfriend. I think once a young woman hits her puberty stage, she should watch this movie. To just understand where love can take you and where love can leave you.

That movie is *Moonstruck*. Starring Nicholas Cage and Cher. One of Cher's best performances if you ask me. And the quote from this movie: ***"Snap out of it*!"** Cher says this after Nicholas Cage kisses her, and tells her that he loves her. She smacks him in the face and yells this quote and leaves. At the end of the movie, she marries Nicholas Cage and everybody lives happily ever after. Just talking about it, gives me a headache. But I love this quote. It really makes you think of what Love is, and what Love can really do to you. It can either give you pleasure, make you feel wanted or it can destroy you. All in one night!

Destroy your heart, your peace of mind forever just for that one more taste of Love. Think of all the songs that are out there for us to listen to. It's all about love. How love hurts, how love can kill your soul if not treated properly. That's it! If Love was treated properly we wouldn't have this kind of trouble. But how can we learn to treat it properly? There are hardly any classes out there that teach you how to treat love properly so that you and your lover can live a happily ever after and never have to quarrel again. Love wouldn't have to be so hard to distinguish EXACTLY which person you are to love, and to spend the rest of your days with that person. Love can give you the greatest power you could never conceive, but it can also crush you like a bug on a windshield.

When a man loves a woman (or when a woman loves a man) their lives just got shattered. They won't be the same, ever. Love corrupts a sane man. That's where that line comes in handy. Sometimes we are so blinded by Love that we aren't quite ourselves. We let ourselves believe that we love a person by their looks, by their apparel, by the way they perform in bed but we never really look deep inside the person. Once you look inside that person's heart, you will then understand them more deeply.

That's what love does. Love helps you get inside the person even if that person has so many walls built around them. We try so many ways to not have someone poking around to find out who we truly are that it's pathetic when something like love can melt those walls around your heart.

Love makes us do so many things that we just don't want to do. Love makes us crazy. Love makes us blind of the other things in life. We don't care if the world is crumbling all around us because we are together! We want to live a life with each other and don't care what you think!! I think that's why Romeo and Juliet was such a huge hit. They found something that melted the walls between them, and they were actually happy with each other even though it broke every law they just learned to live by. But love blinded them. Romeo and Juliet thought that no one would notice.

Let me stop you right there because this is my life story right here. You might not realize this but when you fall in love with someone but you don't really want to admit it, people all around you already can see it and know before even you know yourself that you are indeed in love with that person. Love also blinded them in a way that they didn't realize what this would mean to their families. Love makes you think of only the moment and not what will happen in the future, what your consequences are until you are right on top of them.

That's why I like that movie *Moonstruck*. She was content with that one man, the brother. Was she really truly in love? She thought she was. She thought she was set. Then she met the other brother. She met someone that actually gave her something. Something that no other man has ever given her. But she wanted to keep it civil. She didn't' want to hurt anybody and she didn't want to destroy a great love like the one she had before. But darn that Love. Darn that unstable, maybe I should try it with another man, Love. Once she realized she was in love with the other brother and he loved her, she didn't realize how far that love was. She tried to stop it with a smack, trying to get back to reality, and break that love spell; it was too late.

The spell worked. Love overcame, and it made her blind to what she was doing with her life and it helped her see who she was supposed to be with. You see how tricky love can be? Love just comes in uninvited and sets up a party that will totally destroy you without you even looking, but then it goes and does the nicest thing you can think of. Should you want love in your life? Yes. Is it worth the heartbreak? Yes. Can you learn from love, learn from the mistakes you make while under the influence of love? YES!! It's a great way to show how we really feel about things. The slap also helps too. And that all problems are solved in the Kitchen!

Go forth and re-watch this movie. Which quote do YOU think can help you? And how will this quote help you?

*"**Snap out of it**!"* – Cher in *Moonstruck*

# *November 9, 11:45pm*

## *Day 9*

Just spent another wonderful day with my mother. I have to admit actually, it's a lot of fun spending time with just the two us together. Actually, nothing makes me happier than spending the day with my mother. She brings so much joy out of me, and makes me see things that I really never would have seen in myself. And it's also vice versa with us two. I'll see things about her that she doesn't see or realize and I tell her and show her, and she loves that. She loves that I can see that about her and not be ashamed of it, or embarrassed. I don't think I could have ever been more proud of my mother than those days alone with just her and me together.

When I was growing up, it was mom and I did this, mom and I did that. Many of you know what I mean. Well, most of you. I do know what kind of generation we are and that many of your mothers had to go to work to provide for the family so that usually meant that you never really got the chance to see your mothers, but when you did wasn't it wonderful? Just to be able to sit there and talk with her about YOUR day and about YOUR adventures while she sits there listening to every word you say. It doesn't matter that she had a tough day at the office, as long as she is there to hear your wonderful voice, that's all that counts for her.

With mothers you have that sense of accomplishment. Even though you probably failed at the project, you still feel accomplished for your mother is there to back you up and pick you up when you're down. She knows exactly what to say and when to say it. She knows what to give you and how to present it to you. Fathers; yes of course it is always great to have fathers there to help you to guide you on the right path of life and how to provide for your family, but when it goes down to awarding you, they always give you that "you can do better" "you should have done better" deal. They always want to have a little bit more out of you, but that's expected. They only want what's best for you, so that you can, too, provide for your family. Mothers, they know when to be gentle, they know when to be hard.

They know that giving compliments is the best thing a child needs, and when to give it to them is their specialty as well.

But I believe much of that love and cherish that mother's give their children has been lost over the years. You see so many children these days without their mothers to be there for them, and many times it's not because their mothers are dead. No, no. It's mostly because their mothers are either out there in the world trying to make a name for themselves, or the mothers are so doped on drugs they don't know how to give love to their children.

Many women these days are only getting pregnant for the money. Once they get that welfare checks because they are single mothers, parenting just goes right out the window. It's a sad thing to see parenting go like that. See the children suffering in this world because they never got that giddiness they should have from their mothers when they were children.

Poor choices people are making these days. I'm so fortunate to have a mother that cares for me, and tries to do me right. Many people complement on how mature I am and how polite I am to strangers. They all think I was just born that way. Well, I guess they were right! Just kidding. Mostly it was because of the way my mother raised me, and plus she always said I was an old soul! She raised me to be respectful, to be kind, to be curious, to have ambition for life and to have honor and pride.

Older people are always wondering what's wrong with the children these days. They have parents, they have the giddiness their supposed to get but why the children are still acting bad, like they don't have any respect for themselves or anybody else. The parents aren't quite teaching them that. Ever seen the kids in the store that want a toy? They ask their mother and the mother says no. Ever see the kids? They whine and whine and cry. Of course this is not unusual. Kids do that all the time when they don't get what they want. See what the mother does, though? It sort of makes my point that I'm trying to get across to ya'll. She gives in! She lets her kids have whatever they want. Even after she said no!! Know what that shows the children? That they can get whatever they want and no one can say NO to them. All they have to do is beg, cry, and whine for two seconds and they can get what they want. (Think of our world if everybody thinks that everybody else has to give them what they want? Nobody would get anything done, and everybody will be starving for everybody is waiting on someone to do it for them. How can that be when everybody is not doing anything? Just something to think about.) Now ask yourself this question, why would the mother just give in like that? Why didn't she just stick to her guns and say to the child no and live with the disappointment? Good question. The answer? The mother wants to make friends with their children. They want to give their children everything so that they can be friends and have a wonderful relationship with their children. Well, guess what? ERRRR!!! Wrong-o! The kids have learned one thing of getting everything they want, and their parents WON'T say anything about it: NO RESPECT FOR THEIR PARENTS. If their own parents won't stick up for themselves, then why should the children? That makes no sense for the kids to have respect for themselves and for others when their OWN parents won't.

My mother? Oh no. She stuck to her guns. If I wanted something really really bad and she would say no, I would scream bloody murder till I get it. Think I got it? NOPE. My mother would actually ignore my screams (for she knew what I really wanted), or she would show me something else that I would like that she would be willing to buy, or she would leave the store, leave her groceries and head on home, then ask her husband or her son to pick up the groceries on the way home, but the main point is she would not give in to my screams.

You see folks; she knew if she wanted a relationship with me, she would have to be my MOTHER before she could be my FRIEND. And that's how I was raised. I didn't have a mother as my friend; a friend that would give me anything I needed, comfort me and tell me I was right. No. I had a MOTHER; a woman that corrected me when I was wrong, punished me when I went against the rules, gave me consequences for my wrongful actions, helped me when I was in trouble, guided be through tough times, kissed all my booboos, gave me chicken noodle star soup when I wasn't feeling right. If I was sick, my mother would make me my special kind of soup for me and care for me then she would turn right around and send me to my room with no TV, no books, no music if I did something wrong. She wasn't trying to be my friend; she was trying to be my mother.

Yes, sometimes there were restrictions to some things in my life; yes she was hard on me sometimes, but that's what mothers are for. They are supposed to be hard on you so that you will learn about the aspects of life and get you ready for the time when you are on your own and be able to take care of yourself and then finally a family of your own. She doesn't want her children to be left in the world helpless and undependable. That's not how mothers are supposed to be.

But somehow in the lengths of life, that teaching, that mothering has been lost somewhere and now mothers only want to be their children's friends and not be their mothers. (Why couldn't I had a mother like that? JK LOL). A mother would stop at nothing to protect their children. Would a friend? When a mama bear feels that her cubs are being threatened do you know what they do? They don't ask their children "would you like me to help you" or quietly ever so nicely to tell the others to go away. No, they CHARGE. Without any thought of what will happen to them, they will charge at the attackers and they will do whatever it takes to make sure their cubs are safe again. (That's why whenever you see a cub in the woods, never ever go up to it. You never know where the mother is and you can't quite talk to the mother and reason with her like you would a human. FYI)

Still trying to figure which movie and which quote I chose to use for this day? Well, you would be right to guess that it's about mothers even though it's not Mother's Day. Which movie do you think? I'll help you out, it's an oldie, but with great oldie actors. It's about a man who pretty much is a mean old bastard that would pretty much kill any man that looks at him wrong, but does it all for the sake of his mother. He even said, after he killed a man, and before the cops killed him: ***"Made it Ma. Top of the World."***-James Cagney from *White Heat*. Interesting movie, by the way.

We the people have tried everything to make our parents proud. Ever watch those cop shows that has the victim so psychotic it's hard to watch them go through that and wonder if they are really human or not? Ever see the ending? Most of them are all the same. The psycho's dad, or mother was a crack head and used to beat them up and the psycho is just trying to get the love and respect out of their parents that they never got as a kid. I can't think of anything else that a person would go through to get their love and respect from their parents. If their parents did them wrong, then you can sure bet that all those kids want to do is do something that would make their parents proud. If it's stealing that will get their parents to actually smile to them, then there you go, the kids a thief. If it's killing that will get either one of their parents say "I'm proud of you kid" then you've got yourself a murderer. Sometimes the kids finally get out of the house and into better families and will make better choices and won't have the feeling of trying to make their parents proud of them. They will start making better choices for themselves and not have to worry about if their father is going to beat them again if they don't steal for him. It's a hard world. It's a hard life. People have to get through some really deep (excuse my French) shit to actually do something with their lives.

I think that's why I really enjoyed that movie "*White Heat*". It shows a young man trying to make it in the world, just so his mother would be proud of him, but things were just holding him back. He tries his best to make his mother proud of him that he gets too psychotic about it and that's his life's mission. He can't do anything without thinking of his mother and how his mother would appreciate it.

What does this remind me of? Oh yes, the ENTIRE WORLD!!! Everybody wants to make their parents proud and for many it is the mother that they want to please. Many times it's the father, but it's usually the mother that would give the appraisal they are wanting. In so many ways, I think that is why people do the things that they do; it's all for their mothers. If they don't have anybody to be doing things for, then what's the point? What is there in life if not for that one special someone that will praise them and also prove their love to them. Many will always have that hardwired into them, to be praised by whatever they do by their mothers. Like I mentioned before, why the mothers? Well, my theory is because the mothers are usually the ones that comment on whatever you are doing; they are more likely the ones to give you the appraisal you are looking for where the father would want you to make it look better, push you to do better, to try harder next time. While your mother is on the sidelines as happy as ever even though you lost, she is cheering YOUR name and telling everyone that you are her child. I think that in so many ways, the reason we function, so we can function for our mothers.

We sometimes take mothers for granted, don't we? We always think that they are going to be there forever, forever guiding us to the right direction and also always being there to tell us we did a great job, even though we came in last. But, we have to come to terms that they aren't always going to be there. Time has an away of fooling us from time to time. It may seem just yesterday that mom was holding our hands, and now we're holding her hands saying goodbye as she drifts away. We never want to think about that. We never want to venture into the notion that she will be gone, and we will never get that love back. That's when we lose it. That's when we try so hard to get the comfort, and the appraisal from everyone else, doesn't matter who, as long as we get that appraisal we will then feel content. Not fully satisfying, but able to function. Why? Because of the love and devotion that mothers give, it makes us whole again. It's like we are children all over again, and mother is there holding our hands to comfort us, and tell us that everything is going to be alright. Nobody can give a love like a mother can.

Of course there are other kinds of emotions that mothers have given that makes a child seem lost in the world. Like in this new day and age, where mothers usually get pregnant to only get the child support money, and then don't take care of their children and just do drugs instead. That usually results in a whole new aspect of what our mothers are supposed to do for us, and how we are supposed to obtain this new aspect in life. No mothers to love, no understanding of what things are and how we're supposed to take care of ourselves, and others with the love and devotion we should have gotten from our mothers. With that gone, we take what we can get. Go forth and re-watch this movie. Which quote do YOU think can help you? And how will this quote help you?

*"**Made it, Ma. Top of the world**!"* - James Cagney from *White Heat*

# *November 10, 11:04pm*

## *Day 10*

Just finished watching *The Waltons*. You all remember that wonderful television show don't you? A wonderful story based on the life of Earl Hamner Jr. set during the Great Depression of a family of 7 children in the great state of Virginia that must face hard times but makes it through with love and devotion that they give each other. Ever since I was a little kid I used to watch that show right before I went to school and right after I came home from school. Didn't do a lot for my schooling for I'd be in class wondering what John-Boy Walton would say in situations I found MYSELF in.

In many ways I wanted to be just like him. The whole "being humble" to being down right neighborly to others and being able to write stories like he did. You know the kind that talks about his family and what they did all day long. I wanted to have those same experiences in my po-dunk town. I wanted to be able to write about all the different people and all the different things people did for each other here in my little town. But I just couldn't see it. Since I lived outside of town, I couldn't really venture out on my own for I was the only child in the household and I usually had to help my dad or my mom with chores.

The one thing I really liked about The Waltons was the stories about how John-Boy could recall the details and was able to write them down. I realized that's what I wanted to do. Right then and there, the words grabbed me and I wasn't able to let go. I wasn't able to be set free of that feeling of wanting to write and look at me now. A couple of years go by and I'm trying out for my first writing challenge and I'm already at 14, 041 words. Oh yea, I'm going far.

The other thing that really caught my eye about John-Boy is that even after all the years of being an adult and in college and everything; he still went by that name: John-Boy. Most folks at that age want to be known as grown-ups. John-Boy still had that childish ring to it and even though in his writing he was known as John Walton Jr., he still stuck to his guns and preferred to be called

John-Boy.

Many kids do have that feeling of liking being named after their fathers. They love the notion that their parents would give their first born son the responsibility of passing on the legacy of their name. Kids sometimes feel with the name Junior put on the end makes them stand tall, and they must do whatever it takes to make sure that their name is well known and respected. A whole new generation with that name is now in the hands of the boy and he feels he must not let his father down. It also shows the rest of the town/city or place they are living that the name is being passed on and must be respected. A tradition is being passed on. It's sort of like "Hey, you all know me, now know my son. You can't mistake him, he's the one with Junior painted at the end of his name."

People walking around will know who Junior is and what kind of man he SHOULD be for he is his father's son and has his father's name. Kind of puts a lot of demands on that boy for being called Junior. (Good luck to any Junior's out there reading this.)

Why do you think that so many of the kids these days

DON'T want to be named Junior? Is it because they don't like their fathers? Well, that could be a factor, but I highly doubt it. Is it because they don't want the responsibility? You bet!! Reason? Many reasons why, but I think mostly because kids these days are so afraid of messing up and it tends to be that the road kids are taking they don't want to bring up their fathers name. It's so important to their fathers and to others and the boys don't want to be the ones to mess that up.

But the main reason for boys to NOT be called Juniors? When you are branded with the name of your father, you feel you must act the way he does. You must follow in his footsteps, become the man that he is and try and prove that to other townsfolk. (You have NO idea how much easier it is to be born in the city with millions of people, so that you won't have to feel like this in a small town where everybody knows everybody and gossip is the biggest thing next to American Football.)

But what if that boy wanted to be his own man? What if he had big dreams of his own, and wants to be recognized for himself and not for his father or what kind of a man his father is? Why not just accept the boy as he is and let his old man be who he is and everybody is happy? Because that's not how it runs on good old Walton's Mountain, same as in my po-dunk town. Once you are branded with that title 'Junior' that becomes your beacon of who you must become.

Many have tried to overcome that and move on with their OWN lives, but it always comes back and bites them in the butt. How does one try and get away from the ideal name "Junior"? How can one be established as his own man and not his father?

One man did that, and I believe that's how some of you Juniors out there are living your lives. His name? Well, we all know him as Indiana. To his father: JUNIOR!!

*"**Don't call me Junior**,"* said by Harrison Ford in the movie *Indiana Jones and the Last Crusade* has been a very funny and humorous quote whenever his father, played by Sean Connery, called him Junior. Indiana was so hot mad, he would quote this line every single time. He just wants to be his own man, his own trademark and not to be just like his father. Of course he knows deep down who he is and where he comes from, but to the

world, he's *Indiana*. He's the man that can solve anything, find anything and be anyone. His father had one mission and it nearly took his life and his son's.

The *"**Don't call me Junior**"* I think really brightens up some kids eyes, showing them that they CAN be their own man, they can start out in their own trademarks and not really have to follow so closely in their fathers' footsteps. Now I'm not trying to tell you to never follow your father's footsteps and I'm not trying to tell you to NOT listen to your father. Of course you should listen to him, you should realize he only wants what is best for you, but you can also be your own man. You can make your own choices and it will only reflect on yourself, and not on your legacy.

But I guess the real question is how would you be able to do that without disappointing your father and hurting him while trying to become a man all at the same time? That is difficult to do. For I myself am not a boy, and I am not named after my father. But I do get the sense, the feeling of trying not to offend my father's name. Not knowing how one's family would feel for one's son to not do exactly what his father before him has done, is a little hard for me to imagine. I have seen enough movies and read enough books to understand that it is important to stand for one's own families' beliefs and morals but it is also important for one to stand for his/her own rights and standards of life. That's the choice that God gave each and every one us. If one does choose to follow in his father's footsteps and become like him then all the power to him and pray that God be with him on every step of the way.

But now let's point out that he still is a different man than his father. Like our thumb print; not even twins have the same thumb print that alone makes us all different. For if one boy does decide to go about his way different than his father but still keep the name Junior, then that boy has every right to go his separate way. With his father's blessing or not, Junior has every right to become his own man.

Of course, the way I put this is like I'm trying to tell the fathers out there what to say and what to do about raising their own children. That's not it at all. I'm actually talking to the boys that have grown up all ready but have nowhere else to go for they are lost and confused for they want to be different. But because of so much pride and stubbornness in most men, they lose themselves in what they want to do in life. That's the crowd I'm talking to tonight. I'm trying to tell you men that it is alright to feel like that and want to do good by your fathers. There's nothing wrong in taking your family's name and taking the responsibilities that go along with that, but it should also be said without remorse that you are now living in a new age where you can make your own choices about life and it shouldn't be shame that you feel, but the sense that you have accomplished something by YOUR own name and not your FATHER'S name.

You will see through that stubbornness that your father will be so proud of you, you could share all that pride with hundreds of other men. Just like Senior Jones felt about *Indiana* in the end of *The Last Crusade*. Just don't call him Junior when he doesn't want to be pa, give him that much, eh?

Go forth and re-watch this movie. Which quote do YOU think can help you? And how will this quote help you?

Kelsey Mecher-Wentzloff

# *"Don't call me Junior!"* - Harrison Ford in
# *Indiana Jones and the Last Crusade*

# *November 11, 2012 5:23pm*

## *Day 11*

*"On this Veterans Day, let us remember the service of our veterans, and let us renew our national promise to fulfill our sacred obligations to our veterans and their families who have sacrificed so much so that we can live free."*

~Dan Lipinski.

*"In the beginning of a change, the patriot is a scarce man, and brave, and hated and scorned. When his cause succeeds, the timid join him, for then it costs nothing to be a patriot."*

~Mark Twain

There is so much that can be said about this day. So much sadness, so much remembrance that it hurts. All the families of the soldiers that have died really feel a loss on this particular day for its all people will talk about. If you live in a small town like I do then you will understand, too, how many people can feel so down about this time of year for EVERYBODY is talking about which war they were in, who their buddies were, and what they used to do in the war and how they made it out of there alive while their buddies didn't.

I know it's taken a huge toll on my mother. She was in high school when Vietnam hit. It was very tragic for her for she had seen her friends leave to fight the war. Many came back okay, many came back damaged while other friends never made it back. Her brothers were off in that war as well so she really got a double slap in the face during those years.

I try and understand how that must have felt seeing your friends leave to a whole new world that you haven't heard of except in Geography class. Not really understanding how it could have felt losing many of your friends and family in just one whole year makes it difficult for my mom and me to talk about this subject.

Ever since I could remember, I have been interested in all wars. World War I, World War II, Cold War, Korean War and the Vietnam War, and of course the Gulf war along with the war I am currently living thru, the War on Terrorism (the War in Iraq/Afghanistan ).

I have checked out every single book I could find on all of these wars but more so on World War II and the Vietnam War. Both were very interesting to me when I was little and still are to this day. I have been interested in the battles that took place, the different strategies that the generals took, the way the men fought. It was an extremely difficult time for all of us during those two wars as it is with every war, but with these, you didn't just lose your men in battle but you also lost the souls of the men that returned.

It was a most difficult time during World War II because the Great Depression was just ending. People were starting to get back on their feet, trying to regain what was left of their dignity and move on. Then the war hit. I can't even conceive of how people must have felt losing their families to the Depression and then to lose them to a war.

Then before the Vietnam War, losing our beloved President to a horrible man. We had to draft our boys to go fight a war nobody wanted to fight. Back home families were distraught; people were torn trying to honor their soldiers while fighting against their government to bring back their family members. It was a very difficult 9 years during the Vietnam era where it seemed nobody wanted to fight, and nobody welcomed our soldiers back home for everybody was too high or too drunk to even care anymore. Nine years is a long time; a very long time for families that lost dear friends.

When I had to do a project in school about the Vietnam War I thought I was in heaven. Not only was it my favorite subject to study, but I thought I could ace it with my mom's help. But in fact, it was the most difficult few weeks with her. Not knowing how much it hurt my mom to relive those days was difficult for me to wrap my head around. She understood that I had schoolwork to do so she helped me as much as she could. She brought so much insight on the lives of the women at home that it really helped me to understand the other side of a war.

In school, they taught you the hardships the *men* endured while in battle; how bloody the War had turned, but schools don't really get down to the understanding of how it affected the families that stayed home. Of course, they talk a little bit about how the families at home *helped* the war in many different ways, but never the side of how it killed the mothers to not see their sons for so long. How the wives must have felt all alone, how the girlfriends will never know if their lovers are ever coming back.

It was such a trying time and I tried to wrap my head around it and tried to understand, but I came to the conclusion that if you haven't actually physically lived through it, then you will never truly understand the feelings those woman went through during the wars. Yes, you can see what they did to survive through those trying times, yes you can relate with the deaths like if you had a death in the family yourself you would then understand but you would never truly relate to the pain that those woman went through, what my mother went through knowing that many of her friends would never be coming back. Would never be able to see their smiling faces; to be able to hear their laughter one more time. I will never quite understand how that must have felt. And I hope I never have to.

As small towns go, it's amazing how many stories I

could come up with, for there are many veterans in my small town. Either it would be from The Vietnam War, the Korean War, or even World War II. Very few are from World War I these days, but from the other wars, there are a lot of veterans. Many of them love to sit and talk about those "glory" days some would say, and others just don't want to talk about it. They share some of what they did in the war, but they don't like to dwell in the past. I understand totally. Our town actually has a local WWII vet that loves to talk about what he did in the war, and he even wrote a few books on how a farmer becomes a military man. An interesting read.

I was trying my hardest to find a wonderful quote for this historic day, and a day of remembrance. There are so many lines from movies that I could quote here from many different movies like from *The Longest Day*, *To Hell and Back*, *Sergeant York*, *Faith of My Fathers* and many more.

So many interesting lines about the wars came out of those movies, but I think one of the coolest lines that I think I could use in MY LIFE TIME, would have to be from a movie that you wouldn't consider for Veteran's

Day. A movie that actually talks about war, about the affects it has on people and what people would do in times like these. Instead of it being about one of the bravest soldiers that ever lived, or a General, it's about a man that has more power than a Four Star General: The Commander in Chief himself, the U.S. President.

And what a commander! (In real life, I think he should have run for President if given a chance.) That man is none other than Harrison Ford in his movie *Air Force One*.

Now that is twice in a row that I have used a quote from a movie that Harrison Ford was in and both times it's his line. Of course it's his line, who else could have said it? Harrison Ford has this way of delivering a line that no other actor could or ever will. He puts his whole body into making the line feel solid, like he really means to say this to you and you better pay attention or he'll come after you. LOL. Anyhoo, my favorite part in the *Air Force One* movie is when he's fighting the terrorist in the back of the plane and Ford ejects the man's parachute and states: ***Get Off My Plane.*** That totally was my favorite mostly because he totally took control of his plane again and he was the man in charge and nothing is going to stop him. He took back his possession with the only way available to him: by force. Throughout the whole movie his peers back in D.C. wondered what his actions were based on: was it as a Commander in Chief; as the President of the United States of America; or was he making his decisions as a husband and as a father? Well, in the end, he was all three. Of course, he made many decisions as a husband and as a father because let's face it folks, he put his family first, he loves them so dearly, who would blame him?

But then when he said *Get off my plane*, which made you as the viewer notice that, he was thinking as a military man as well as a family man. He used both his love and his faith towards getting what he loves most in life, his family, and his possession of the Presidential plane. And if you want a deeper (psychological) look into things, I actually think he was speaking about his plane metaphorically. Using his plane, that belongs to the United States of America, as THE United States of America. When saying *get off my plane,* I think he meant "get off of my land; this is my territory and you just aren't welcome. So GET OUT!!" His possession was the plane, but it was also what the plane stood for. Think about it…that plane flies the President around. The President is man (or woman) IN CHARGE of the United States. He is the head of our government and our military, the buck stops with him. (Bully for you, Mr. President!!!) And Air Force One is the plane that flies him around and when he is in another country that plane stands for America. So, when Harrison Ford states "*Get off my plane*", he's really speaking "Don't mess with America."

So now that's pretty much how I can use this quote in the aspects of MY own life. I mean, I'm not the President, I'm not that important, like I don't have a title or anything, so how can I, a puny little middle class woman, use this quote to enlighten my life and make my life much better?

Honestly? I have no idea. I mean, I can't say this to anybody without really meaning it, like get off my land before I shoot you down, or whatever, but yeah, how can I relate this to my life, so then you can see how it can relate to your life? Mostly I think I can probably use this line if someone is taking over my airplane (yes, I can pilot an airplane) and I have the chance to actually throw someone out the window, or hold them in the terminal and then throw them away. But I think I would actually be using the metaphor that this line was intended for.

If someone would be interested in ruining my way of life I can use this statement, this metaphor and use it to my best interest. Not so much as saying it, but remembering what it stood for. The meaning behind the statement is really actually what I would use. The right to protect what you believe in, the right to do what it takes for the things and people that you love. If it comes to violence, then it must be taken care of, but try to use that as the last resort. It may feel like we're all fighting the biggest war ever, but that war is between you and yourself; try not to bring the world squished between it.

If I am ever in this kind of situation, I'll remember this line; remember what it stands for and how Ford delivered it. Why remember how Harrison Ford delivered the line? Because, it was the best line ever delivered in that movie and the look on his face when he said it. I can smile after all the bad that happens. Have to be able to laugh about this whole thing or I would just go crazy.

Go forth and re-watch this movie. Which quote do YOU think can help you? And how will this quote help you?

*"**Get off my plane**."* – Harrison Ford in *Air Force One*

# *November 12, 4:15am*

## *Day 12*

Life is like a maze, a trap, a place full of secrets, a place of illusions and mystery. Come to think of it, life is sort of like those pictures on the back of MAD Magazine. You remember those, right? They'll have a picture, and if you fold it right it spells out the answer to the mystery. Life is like that picture most of the time. All distorted, doesn't make any sense at all at first, then when all the stars align and the picture is folded in all the right places, you will finally find the answers that you are looking for.

And the way to get out of that type of maze is smarts, guidance, and understanding. We all have those traits; we just need to figure out how to use them correctly. Like saying *Abracadabra!!!* But in this day and age we don't have those special magic wands to wave around to make things work in your favor. Nor are there any special words that can be said to make things work when you want them too.

Wait....I lied. There are special words that can help you along the way. Sometimes they work sometimes they don't, well, not to your satisfaction that is. At least, when you say them it kind of gives you a boost like it will work....trust me it will work. Whatever you're striving for, whatever career you want to get into, no one can stand in your way.

For some reason or another, people in this world love to criticize. It's sort of like a turn on for some, to see others suffer, to see others try as hard as they can to make it in this world with no direction and watch them fail over and over again.

Many of you are on this path right now. You're going along in life, just taking one step at a time but you have no idea where you're going or where the path will lead you. What movie can help you now? Well, this is the kind of weird movie to think of when everything in your life, in your path, is going downhill that you would actually NEED to watch this movie to get the gift of this quote. It actually helps. TRUST ME! I've done it. I'll be walking along, and something someone said to me comes to mind or I'll see something that reminds me of where I'm heading (spiritual or literal) and I'll say this line and it works. I'm so much better and I can actually keep walking down my pathway in life and actually accomplish the things I need to get done. The magical words to get through the doors to Narnia are: *"**Go that way really fast. If something gets in your way, turn**"*, said by Curtis Armstrong in *Better off Dead*. A truly hilarious movie that actually has a message about life and what to do about it. A story where this teenage boy played by John Cusack gets dumped by his girlfriend who he thought was the love of his life, because she wants to get popular. Does he take it well? Of course not, he's a teenager. So he tries to think of ways of killing himself and everyone always end up in disaster: to people around him!

He tries everything to get his girlfriend back and if that means killing himself in a skiing race then so be it. His friend played by Curtis Armstrong tries with all his might to confuse Cusack about what his life really means to the people around him. And he says this line to confuse Cusack even more and I guess not realizing how much this line can impact people 26 years later!!

So what is so important about this line? Why would anyone in their right mind want to say this while walking down a crowded street? Mostly we want to reach the end of the tunnel. Trust me, you of all people should know what you want most, right? You want to be able to get to the finish line and accomplish things that others said you could never do. You want to be able to follow those dreams of yours and actually accomplish something in your life. That's all we ever wanted. If you look at each and every scholar, professor, police officer, military, writer, actor, all they ever wanted was to accomplish something, and be acknowledged for it. But the funny thing about life is that things can get in your way. Let's see if we can identify what those "things" are.

"Things" are different for each individual person. I'll use me as an example of how "things" can get in your way and distract you from your destiny, or in other words what you want to do in life. When I decided I wanted to write, I was overjoyed. I was coming up with ideas, great ideas for stories. Great ideas for my blog sites. Everything was going great. Then I hit two of my "things" that got in the way of me actually finishing ANY of my projects. Entertainment was one. People were the other.

Entertainment: Ahh, the joy of watching other people's actions through tough times, seeing them search for the right answer is a comfort. Because I can actually use those answers in my daily life. (Hence the reason for this book J) The problem? I like watching movies ALL THE TIME. Especially TV shows. I have the NCIS, Castle, Supernatural and The Andy Griffith Show DVDs so I am constantly watching reruns of my favorite episodes. I actually know every line in a Bob Hope Bing Crosby television show. It's cool but then scary at the same time. I mean, is this what my life has become? When I was in school this was a problem. I would watch TV instead of doing my homework, so when the tests came around, I couldn't remember what we talked about. But you ask me what Fred Astaire was singing to Ginger Rogers in Top Hat, and I know all the lines he said and even the lyrics to the songs.

And where exactly is that going to get me in life? Is that going to pay the bills? Pay for the food on the table?

Pay for the roof over my head? Reciting old lines. Not really. Yes I am writing a book about old lines now, but I wasn't then. That's the whole point. I was just doing it for fun but failing in school. Entertainment got me away from my studies and it kept me from writing.

Then the people. Oh, people are such joys when it comes to standing in your way of your dreams. Funny thing is I don't know why. As I said beforehand I am not a professor, I am no psychologist, so this topic is beyond my reach. (Paging Dr. Phil...Dr. Phil are you in the house?) I don't really know what makes people tick in certain ways, and honestly I don't think I want to venture down that road. I don't even think the philosophers are 100% accurate. We will never really fully understand the mind, but we do have to live with the knowledge people will do what people want to do. If it's to go to the moon, they will go. If it's to be the smartest person in the whole dang planet, then we have Einstein and all those that follow him. If it's to write a kick-ass book, then by golly we will have books. If it's to shut down a person's dream because they don't want others to succeed if they can't, then by golly they get right in front and destroy those dreams from ever coming true.

It's sad really. To know that we humans actually think like this. To know that people will backstab you, lie to you, deceive you so THEY get theirs, it's just so wrong. But it's been going on since creation began and there's no stopping it, no matter how much money you have invested.

So how do WE get around those lies, those "things" that will distract us from what we want to do? There are many different ways to do this and it's up to YOU to find a way around it. For everyone is different and will have different ways to achieve your goals. One way to help is remember this quote. *"Go that way really fast."* Yes in the movie Armstrong is talking about skiing but let's applies it to our lifestyles. You want to achieve your goal so go for it, head on and really fast. Try and collect all things that will make it happen for your life. *"If something gets in your way, turn."* If those "things" those people that "get in your way" appear, turn. Don't fight. Don't try to reason your way around it, because trust me you will lose. I don't care if you are a teacher, person with an IQ higher than Einstein, Dr. Phil or even

Rambo reading this book, you will lose this fight. Just…turn.

Think of the movie…life comes at you fast; you're heading in your chosen direction and all of a sudden there is a tree standing in your way.  What do you do?  Stop?  You can't, you're going too fast. Even if you stop, you'll crash right into the tree.  Try and reason your way through?  Dude, it's a freakin' tree!  You can't reason your way through a tree.  Turn? Yes!  The only way around a tree, a wall of snow, a boulder is turn and keeps going on your pathway. You're just coming from a different direction but you'll still end up at your destination.

So you're skiing down a long hill really fast. Something gets in your way, what do you do?  You turn. Apply that to life, and you will have your personal Olympic Gold Medal.

Go forth and re-watch this movie.  Which quote do YOU think can help you?  And how will this quote help you?

*"Go that way really fast.  If something gets in your way, turn."* – Curtis Armstrong in *Better off Dead*

# *November 13, 4:14pm*

## *Day 13*

So many movies, so little time!! Literally, I mean that. There are so many movies to choose from that might have some meaning behind them that would be perfect for this book. It seems such an impossible task to accomplish right now, but amazingly for the last 17 days I have been able to pick a movie; write about the day using that line as my inspiration, and still have time to watch other movies.

Like right now I'm watching a great classic! A classic movie for every boy and girl to watch. Steven Spielberg really out did himself on this one. He put a lot of time and effort to make sure that this movie would become a classic and for many years to come people would still be watching this movie. Who wouldn't want to watch about the first Alien sighted in America and how it took the strength and the love of one 10-year old boy to make sure that this Alien makes it safely home?

Yes, folks. I am talking about *E.T. The Extra-Terrestrial*; one of the greatest Alien movies of all time. This movie made Aliens spectacular. This movie made Aliens something to look forward too. This movie taught us what Aliens can be, and maybe what they are. Every night I would look up at the stars and think "Is E.T. coming back? Maybe I should leave out some Reese's Pieces for him, just in case." Oh yea, I bet you all did that once in your lifetime. Don't lie. It's okay. Let it out. I'll say it for you...'Yes, Kelsey. I dropped Reese's Pieces all over my backyard so I could meet E.T'. Aren't you glad to get that out of your system?

*E.T.* really brought out the kid in you. Made you think of what you are capable of doing for someone else that you love and at a very young age. Whether that would be a family member, a friend, even a stranger that you just met at your local grocery store: You were there for them. And in turn, they will be there for you. You have that sense of security in your life that if you mess up in something, someone is always there to help you, to comfort you and to guide you along the way.

And usually that someone is a loved one. Mother, Father, close Aunt or Uncle. Grandparents are always a wonderful choice to help guide you along your way, for they have been there and done all that.

Many times it's a mentor from school: Coach, Teacher, Counselor, and Principal. It's always a joy when kids find their mentor, their 'someone' to help guide them along the way so that they   won't have to do it on their own.

It's a tough world out there and if these kids are not prepared to meet life head on, well, they'll get crushed like a bug on a windshield for not being prepared. The world will try to crush you down, and if you don't have someone watching your back, you'll fall down on your ass before you know it. When you have someone watching your back, knowing that you can go to them anytime for advice.....

For me it's my Mom AND my Dad. They both have literally been there and done most of all that so I know if I have any questions about an ordeal going on and they are giving me advice I know that's from history, from their own past. I always know that they will be there for me and that I can depend on their advice. Hopefully, you have found that someone who you can go to and they will help you in any way that they can.

But what if that special someone wasn't there anymore? What if your mother, father, grandparent, mentor (god forbid) died? In many ways, that's how many of these kids in this day and age are having to fight their way through this crummy world alone because their mentor or family members died. Now they have no one to go to, no one to get advice from. They feel all alone, they feel cheated in their life and now they are left to figure things out for themselves.
Who will be their hero now, is what often goes through their mind when they lose someone like that. They feel all lost and alone, looking for something that they can believe in, looking for something that they can do with their life. Sound familiar?

That John Denver song *Sweet Surrender* really ties into what I'm talking about. In the song he talks about you being on your own, you're trying to do something with your life, and you need to know and understand that living in the now is something worth fighting for and to live your life to the fullest.

Denver knew that many have no idea where they're heading, but to know that there is a "spirit" that will guide you. A "light that shines for me" is another way he puts it.

What does that mean? In many ways, it is a Spirit, the Spirit from God that is watching over you and helping you in the time of need. Now if you're a Christian, you believe in this, if you not, then look a little deeper into your soul and your heart when you're thinking about doing something, or thinking about this road to take in your life and you will hear another voice.

Now I'm not talking about a deep *James Earl Jones* voice telling you where you should be going, but a secondary voice letting you know if this road is alright or if it isn't. In a lot of ways it is God filling in those questions for you, but if you pay attention to the voice who does it sound like? For me, it's my mother. Now thankfully my mother is still alive so I can actually go down the road and asks her for advice, but lately I have been on my own here as I moved out of the house and am living on my own. So it'll be a while before I get any advice in person on some choices I make in my life.

Interesting enough, whenever I am about to make a choice on something, I hear this little voice in the back of my mind telling me I shouldn't because of this, or, yea, great choice! And that little voice? It's the voice of my mother. Telling me, guiding me, and counseling me.

Look into your life real quick. Ever had that feeling where you were about to do something in life and you're not quite sure if this is the right thing to do, ever hear that little voice in the back of your head that guides you along the way? Don't lie to me! I'm an author; I can see the lie right on your face! You've had that voice go "Hey!!! NO NO!! That's not right!" Or, "Oh sure, go ahead. No prob. We get in trouble we get in trouble. No Biggie!!" Whose voice is that? Listen carefully. It's that special someone who was your mentor through all those years growing up.

It's either your Parents, Grandparents, Teacher whoever was your mentor. You are trying to find out where you are going in life, their voice will pop out and you will still have that "spirit that guides me" feeling. And people are like, "How can this be?" Simple. Think of what E.T. was telling Elliot at the end of the movie. *"I'll...Be...Right...Here"*. Where was he pointing? Ohhhh....LIGHTBULB!!! He was pointing at Elliot's head. Wherever Elliot ended up, wherever the road of life took him, he will always remember E.T. He will always remember his voice, his mannerisms, because E.T. will always be in his life whether he took off for his home planet, died of some disease or whatever, they will always have that bond that can never be broken. That's the same type of bond that you have with your loved one or your mentor.

I see so many people down in the dumps after a loved one dies or moves away. I was the same way when my Grandfather died. And he was my favorite friend in the whole world. He could do things no one else could do. He could make me laugh till I peed in my pants he was so darn funny. And when he died, it was the hardest blow I ever took. I couldn't understand why someone who is loved by all had to die. It was hard for me. He would never see me graduate; never see me take flying lessons; never read my writings.

It was tough for me to realize that my best friend

wasn't going to be there for me, to give me guidance when I needed it the most. Some of you are probably going through that right now over a lost loved one. Not sure where to go from here for you know for certain that that loved one will never be able to see you smile or to help you in any way, shape or form. I was the same way. Till I heard this quote. I was babysitting my neighbor's kids and they wanted to watch *E.T.* while eating hot dogs, so after I got done making the hot dogs, we plopped ourselves down and started watching the movie. Right at the end of the movie, when *E.T.* looked at Elliot and said *I'll...Be...Right...Here* it hit me. WHAM!! Just like that. When I finally got home I had more to think about what I just watched. *E.T.* was not just an alien, someone who is lost and needs help. No, *E.T.* was more a friend to Elliot than anything else. Elliot was right there the whole time and tried to help out a friend. Now that friend must venture back home which is like a million miles away and they will never see each other again. When *E.T.* says this, to me it's like insurance; insurance that even though they are miles apart, they will always be together for their heart and their mind won't let them forget their friendship.

Your mind is an amazing tool in your body. It helps you to remember things that are the most important in your life and your heart is filled with that love, that assurance of that friendship that will never die.

*"I'll...Be...Right...Here"* is an assurance that no matter what happens in life, no matter what the future has in store, you will always have that love that does have a meaning and you don't have to do it alone. Because you are never alone.

Go forth and re-watch this movie. Which quote do YOU think can help you? And how will this quote help you?

*"I'll...Be...Right...Here*" – Pat Welsh in *E.T. The Extra-Terrestrial*

# *November 14, 2:25pm*

## *Day 14*

Love *luv* noun: deep affection; fondness. beloved one; sweetheart. sexual passion. delight in; admire. greatly cherish.

These are all great definitions of what love means according to Webster. Many people have many different definitions of what love is, what love entails and what culture has taught us over the years. Each human being has a different feeling towards love. We all have different aspects of what love will do in our lives. From how much it will change everyday lives to how much we will have to adjust to accommodate love.

I've actually had a hard time with this quote. Mostly because there are so many other quotes that I have already written about love, so why is this quote special? I could have picked other quotes as there are millions to billions of quotes to choose from. But as I was talking with friends and online friends, this quote speaks volumes. Interesting that when asked about this quote, the first response has always been the same: eyes rolled towards the heavens, that reluctant heavy sigh and the readyforthatorgasm smile! Either it's for the hot guys that appear in this movie or the quote itself; it really has an effect on women. (Men, remember this quote! It could help you with your wives!!)

No, seriously though. How can this one quote fill you up with the deepest of affections, the sexual passions towards one another? And how can I compare them to the "other" love quotes that I have already written about? I swear, I think all I'm doing right now is writing a love book filled with cupid's quotes to you all, when I'm trying to write down quotes from movies that will actually help you with your day to day lives! How did that happen? How can this book go a whole 360° without me realizing it? I'm the one writing the dang book, I should be the first one to realize it, not the last!

So, I guess my question is why? Why is my book mostly about love? Many of the "love" quotes are for couples just starting out, or couples that have been at it for years but have lost the zing in their relationships or between families. Why is that? Why would Hollywood waste all of their financial investment on movies and T.V. shows to portray love to people, and for *years*? They have been doing this since the dawn of time. Shakespeare? All about love; twisted love, yes, but still love.

So how can Hollywood, movie stars, and writers spend all of their precious time, their late hours, studying the lines over and over and the bottom line comes to: Love? Sort of makes you think that Hollywood is trying to hint to people what love means. Love's definition to the whole world brought to you by the big screen, coming to a home theatre near you! It's like Hollywood is seeing how people don't quite understand the full meaning behind love and they wish to portray that love so people will know and understand love and do a better job at it.

But we are intelligent people; we have been *making* love for century's now--- I think we get the picture. We all went to high school, we all saw the films. We know what it is and how to achieve it, right?

Then I watch the news. I see my neighbors. I see

the families. I see my own family. I see the shelters. I see the cops. I see the bruises, the hurt, and the betrayal. That's when I see it. That's when I understand. That's when it all makes sense.

I see how people treat each other and it just disgusts me. It disgusts me to know that a supposed 'loved one' could do harm to another. That there is no more feelings for love, no more "wanting" love. Just taking it. Then it hits me. Hollywood is trying to showcase what love is and what love can do to us. That's the reason for finding so many quotes that showcase love. It's like they're trying to help us all out about love. And like I said before, I have already written about love and how to get it, let's talk about how to keep it. How not to lose it and how to keep it "alive" as they would say. And there is only one quote that I know of that works perfect for those that are losing their "spark". The ultimate perfect quote that people should say to each other is "*P.S. I Love You*."

There was something in the way Gerard Butler said it to Hilary Swank in the movie *P.S. I Love You* that really got to me. Not just because he has that sultry voice and that amazing accent of his, but what the words really mean. The way this world has turned out, we all could use this quote more often than not. People need that reassurance that they are STILL loved by many.

Whether it be from a family member or from a companion. So lately Hollywood needed to show what love is supposed to be for couples. They hope that people would actually apply that into their lives. Unknowing that there were already people that understood what I Love You, really means.

Here's an example that I hope will help you in your life:

"Martha and Richard"

Married for 47 years.

First look was all it took.

Most wonderful family, amazing friends.

A good life.

Not a care in the world, just for each other.

Through the good times, through the bad times.

Always together, never apart. P.S. I Love You.

Then the doc's long face tore all that apart.

It takes meetings with many different doctors saying different things. A case of IVs start to rule their world,

RNs and ICU are their new safe words; vending machines their source for breakfast, lunch and dinner.

Hospital staff knows them by their first names, greeting them like in Cheers. Friends come and goes, family calling first chance they get. Visiting hours are over: P.S. I Love You.

Then it's the coughing. Always starts with that. Then it goes downhill from there. Moving from one room to another. From one state to another chasing treatments upon treatments. Don't remember what home is for the meds are home now. Going from crosswords puzzles to Sudoku, to what's happening to that movie star that you never heard of before.

Learning the medical lingo is like learning how to speak again. Beeps going off left and right; just want to take a .22 to it! Visiting hours are over: P.S. I Love You.

Finally the docs know what it is, but nothing more they can do. Let's try this drug, let's try the chemo. Let her rest, get her blood moving. P.S. I Love You.

Broth is the new beverage. Jell-O shots at 2:30 in the morning is the new fav!! But moving the insides take more time than usual. Eyes are upon you as you take that last dump. Scarier now that a stranger has to help you in and out of bed. Never want to see that gloved hand approach you again. P.S. I Love You.

Then the even longer face sets things off. You just hit rock bottom from the hill and no way back up. Talk of Hospice, talk of just going home for the final run. Choices, choices, choices. P.S. I Love You.

Docs say its time. No way you're leaving her side. Stick the rules of visiting hours where the sun don't shine, she won't be left alone. Doc gives the final word; family is looking out for her best interest. "I'm sorry honey. See you up in heaven. P.S. I Love You."

This quote has meant more than some chick flick movie could make it out to be. This saying brings more than just tears in the eyes. It can bring a smile to one's face about how much love one man can show to his companion during such a trying time and also to the couples that still have each other and can resurrect the spark again... just by saying those words: ***P.S. I Love You***.

Go forth and re-watch this movie. Which quote do

YOU think can help you? And how will this quote help you?

> ***"P.S. I love you"*** – Gerard Butler from *P.S. I Love You*

# *November 15, 7:30pm*

## *Day 15*

Fifteen days of just writing. Writing anything that pops into my head and needs to be put on paper.

My knight in shining armor has done it. He has made me into a writer. I'm writing like none stop; anything I see at the library that looks interesting enough, I'm writing about it; I hear a song on the radio and I'm like "Oh, I could write a story based on this song", I write it down.

MY FINGERS ARE TIRED!!!! Many would be writing their stories down with pen/pencil on paper like so many other authors have done. Many will use their typewriters (if they are still out there) and others would use the new technology out there and use a laptop. I'm part of the majority that uses their laptops/computers to get the job done. But fifteen straight days of typing, of storytelling on things that just pop into my head: Can anyone say Band-Aids and Tylenol?!!!!  But I'm not complaining (much) but it has been effective.  Look how many quotes I have already finished.  Fourteen good quotes; fourteen great movies that we all love and cherish along with adding them to your lifestyle for your function of living.

And many we have already added to our life we just didn't realize it.  You're going along in life, things aren't exactly working out like you planned but then you remember what your favorite actor or actress did/said in a movie that portrayed what you're going through at the same moment and you remember what they said and how they got through it.  And without you knowing it, you used a quote from your favorite movie and applied that in your lifestyle.  Easy to slip into that isn't?

Well, I guess that's one of the reasons why I chose to write about my favorite movies and my favorite quotes and share them with you and tell you how they have had such an impact on mine and my family's lives.

That's got to be something for the actors and actresses who said these lines in movies to know that what they said, what they did in the movies really touched many people out there in the world. It's not just some acting job, some job to get money from but it's reaching out to the people that are struggling in life and trying to find who they are and where they are going and these actors/actresses have shown them a possibility in life. They have got to be feeling proud of themselves that through their movies they have inspired many people to go out there in life and actually live because of one movie.

Interesting that that's how our society will grow. That how we have taught our children is that movies are the pathways in life and for many movies and TV shows are used as teaching tools to the young to understand more of their culture and about themselves. Huh.

The above paragraph was pretty much me explaining my actions here as I'm writing. It's letting you know why I'm writing this book, and it's also letting my brain know why my fingers are cramping up and why I've lost all feeling in my buttocks. It has nothing to do with the next quote I am about to present, though.

In all actuality this next quote is going to be fun for me to write. It's actually my favorite quote from my favorite movie. I have actually looked at the aspects of my life and every else's life around me.

Ladies and Gents of all sizes, *The Princess Bride* enters from stage left to show you what I mean. And no it's not "Inconceivable" or "As You Wish." But a quote that everyone will know, that everyone will relate to and that everyone will love. ***"Hello. My name is Inigo Montoya. You killed my father. Prepare to die."*** said by Mandy Patinkin as Inigo Montoya, one of the greatest Spaniards that ever walked the face of the Imaginary World.

A strong man; a man that will do anything in his power to achieve his goal. He has proven to us in the movie what one man will do to accomplish his mission. Even though he's laughed at; he's used for things that he doesn't believe in; he's ridiculed for what he believes in, and yet through all the trials and tribulations this man goes through, he still goes after the 6-finger man that killed his father because he has sworn an oath to avenge his father's death.

He showed many people in the movie and to the people that were watching the movie that even though he endangered his life; even though he was laughed at and thrown out of every town and home he knew; he was committed to make sure that his father's honor will live on. That his father won't die in vain; that his legacy will live on through Inigo and Inigo must show this by proving himself and killing the man who killed his father.

Now come to think of it, nobody really talks like that anymore. Nobody really thinks that way. This is a shame. A real shame if you think about it. In this new generation, we have lost that part of our culture. The culture of making sure our families legacy of honor is still strong, and still growing. In this new day and age, we the people don't even think about the possibility of losing one's honor in one's family and we don't even understand what the importance of one's honor if lost; we won't even care! That's sad!

I just have to say it. It used to be a culture where kids tried to protect their honor, their families' names. They would do almost anything to make sure that their father's name was not tarnished in any way. One would be like Inigo Montoya: sacrificing his life and his time to become the greatest swordsman in the world JUST to kill the man with the six fingers. He didn't just do it to look good to others, like so many of these kids today.

Everything in this new lifetime is one soap opera after another. People these days will only do things that will make them stand out in the crowd! Not Inigo Montoya. No, not him. He stood his ground for his father even when all were laughing at him.

Could you do that? Would you be able to lay down YOUR life; give up everything you own, all the toys that you spent hundreds on just to honor's one name?

Before you say yes, think for just a minute. Would you truly honor your name? Would you truly if all else fails; you would just pick yourself right up and still go after the thing you seek? Are you capable of doing that? And do you also have the strength to do that? That's what gets me. In the year 2011, most American teenagers don't give a crap about their legacies. It's sort of like they don't care if their name is ruined by someone's rumors or by their own carelessness. They don't care anymore. It makes you wonder who's at fault here doesn't?

That I can tell you, and it pains me to say this. But

it's from all the upraising these new generations are getting from home. Either their father is off work 24/7 every week so they don't get the guidance that a father should be showing. Or their mother is lying on her back either it's for work or it's because she's flat out high/drunk. Either way the children have to fend for themselves and when they get older and see that their families are nothing but pieces of trash loitering around the cities then they don't care about "one's honor' when one doesn't even have an honor to speak of.

And if one does have a family that has many reputations it's mostly getting high and being stupid or it's their mother's lying on their backs a lot. It pains me to see that that is how our society has gotten. That's how FAR we have let it go on. It needs to stop. We need more Inigo Montoya characters walking around cities "Gibb slapping" everyone into getting them to wake up and smell the coffee!!

This line always touches me. Not only because it's funny; you remember how he keeps saying it over and over and over while killing the six-finger man but it's also something that we can say as well.

You're going along in life and you need a boost. Things are just not going your way: bills haven't been paid, the report that was due last week is still not finished, and you're arguing with your spouse, AGAIN!!!

Then all of a sudden you see a sword pop up out of nowhere. You pick it up. You seize the opportunity and you scream out at the top of your lungs: "Hello. My name is Inigo Montoya. You killed my father. Prepare to die." Say that a few more times and you will actually see a smile cross your face. Trust me: A FREAKIN' SMILE J

You won't be able to stop; you'll just keep going and going and going till you can't take it anymore. Then THAT'S when you are ready to face your boss; THAT'S when you face your bills with a smile.

You'll be able to stand tall again, hold your head high, and you will keep your honor and your name in good fortune again! If that doesn't make your blood boil, then I don't know what will!!!

Go forth and re-watch this movie. Which quote do YOU think can help you? And how will this quote help you?

*(And for those that are reading this, if you don't understand about keeping your families honor and respect, then I will personally come down and give you a Gibb slap.  Understand?!?!)*

**"Hello.  My name is Inigo Montoya.  You killed my father.  Prepare to die."** - Mandy Patinkin in *The Princess Bride*

# *November 16, 5:45pm*

## *Day 16*

In many of these latest quotes, I have written about finding your love; love between families mostly love between you and your parents; the love of yourself.

But I have not yet written about the things you must do when you have found that love, when you have committed to the one man or one woman in your life. And I'm not going to. I'm not going to give you the answers you are looking for when and after you get married. That's for you to find out and discover for yourself. And even if I would help you and tell you what the answers are, I wouldn't be a very good source for it. I'm not even married, so how could I give you the answers you seek?

But, I do want to help you in any way I can to either "fix" your marriage or just help your marriage go on an easier track.

This next quote is mostly for the woman to read, to think about, and digest on what this quote means to them, but men don't go putting this book down just yet. This quote is sort of...how can I put it? A warning? Would that help me? To say that this quote is a warning to you before you get married, so that when you are arguing (and trust me you are going to argue) with your spouse that you will reflect on this quote and understand that the woman is always right. (Happy Wife, Happy Life!) No, that was not the quote, but it goes with the sentiment I'm trying to build here.

So, without further ado, Ladies and Gentlemen, those of you that are planning on, already are, or just wanting to read something on a rainy afternoon, a quote that will make men understand women better; a quote that will make women understand how to run their household without making their wonderful beautiful hair turn to gray. The quote is: *"**The man is the head, but the woman is the neck. And she can turn the head anyway she wants.**"*

This quote is from none other than that great movie I mentioned beforehand (you, the one that's just flipping through this book at a drugstore, check out the contents one more time and you'll see what I mean) *My Big Fat Greek Wedding.* This time it's from the Mother who is played by Lainie Kazan, a wonderful woman who should be idolized throughout history.

Anyhoo…I can already see the ladies smiling over this. It is so perfect for women to live by and to remember when they get married. I can also see the men scratching their heads, saying huh? It's very simple: the men keep claiming that they are the head of the house; decisions are left to him to make; everything goes by him; the young man that wants to take the father's daughter's hand in marriage must go through him, and HE sets the rules of the house and they must be followed or there will be consequences.

The woman is there to make sure that HIS rules are followed, and there is order in the house when he is off to work. That's how it USED it be!! Back then, that's how the men were treated in their own homes. They were treated with authority and everything was left to him to decide how things were accepted or not accepted. Old movies show you that men make the decision, and the woman just sits idly by and does nothing but nod. In real life, well. That's a whole other story.

What we never realized is that the woman behind the scenes is the person that ran everything. Women have proven over and over that they are the more superior, smarter and more stubborn as years go by. It's hard to be a woman in a man's world, but somehow we women have proven that we are capable of taking anything at face value, and still keep our posture up and our game faces on so that the children won't be hurt.

Ask the men if they could do that? And still get dinner ready on the table! There is a joke out there that states that Jesus was actually a woman. Why? He fed a crowd at a moment's notice when there was no food; He kept trying to get a message across to a bunch of men who just didn't get it; And even when He was dead, He had to get up because there was work to do! That actually makes sense now that I think about it. But the Bible said He will do great wonders, so it's a man but that also sums up a woman's life for you. She has to do all that to make sure the kids stay straight, and that her husband is on the straight and narrow path and not making a total fool of himself.

The last part always gets me: trying to keep "her" man on the straight path and stopping him from doing something that would make him look foolish, and it's her job to do that? That never made sense to me. I mean, the man is the head of the family; he is in charge; he knows his boundaries, he's a grown man. He can take care of himself. Then I actually look out there and see all the men that have crossed my path and I'm like, "Oh yea. They really need us woman to keep them straight!"

But it's also the way many of the woman show their affection towards their husbands that astound me. They don't yell at them in front of their friends; women don't hit their men in front of their family; women don't scold them like a little child in the store (of course they do act like children at many times). That's for when they get home or in the car and THEN the scolding starts. Am I right men? If you said no, then you need to look at your woman, look at the last few lines, back to your woman, back to the lines and then you better look at your woman and say to her Thank You. Then turn to the book and say Thank you Miss Kelsey. Your wife will understand.

(Believe me; they already read this book once!)

The reason that most women won't do the things I listed is because they love their man, they want to keep their man, and they don't want to look like they belong to their man if their man seems to act like a child! (They can run away very fast if their lives depended on it: even in high heels!)

The scene that has this line in it just makes my day. If it's alright I would like to share the scene with you. It'll only take a moment, and hey! It's my book.

Toula is trying to get her dad to let her go to school so that she can learn more about computers. When her father won't let her, she thinks that's it! What he says goes, "he's the man, and he's the head of the house." Then our line. Then how does she go about using her "power" that Toula has no idea her mother had? Well, for that you will have to see the movie. You'll see the part, can't miss it.

I can tell you this....it was beautifully done. Even though Maria knows that it means so much for him to be the head of the house and what he says goes and she also understands that he hates to see his little girl all grown up and yes possibly leave him. Maria knows all of this and yet she argues with him, why? Because she knows what it would mean to Toula, the knowledge that she has could expand and she doesn't want to see that demolished because her father "doesn't want to see his baby girl grow up." No way will a Mother stand in the way of her little girl expanding her knowledge.

Now if this means getting into an argument with her husband then so be it. But she also makes it and lets her kids see that it was HIM that had the idea, that it was HIM that changed his mind, (Although the kids always know it's mother that makes things happen) just to make it look like the father still is in control and still the head of the family.

See that's the difference between the man and the woman when it comes right down to taking care of the children. The Father: he wants to make sure that his children are living in the moment, they are taken care of and that they are financially okay. The Mother: wants to make sure that her children can take care of themselves that they will know that they can expand their knowledge and she will teach her children that no matter what people say, they can do anything that they set their hearts to. Difference: Mothers understand that the children want to grow up, that they want to do things for themselves where as the Father looks into doing it himself and doesn't want his children to grow up and leave the house just yet.

A study from a college states: "The bond each human being nurtures with their mothers is irreplaceable. Every man on earth, irrespective of their ethnic and cultural background and upbringing, will bear testimony to this fact. Women are the first educators of children and have that special connection with the offspring of this world. It is women who give birth to children and not men. This fact alone makes the superiority of women a deserving title that men can never ever manage to challenge, let alone achieve, even in the wildest of their dreams."

Women are the world's most successful "multi-taskers". There is a book out there that states that men process life like waffles. They think and act by moving from box to box just like waffles are made. They enter into a box, look at the problem and then come up with a solution. But they can only do one box at a time.

Woman, on the other hand, process life like a plate of spaghetti. Each issue is like an individual noodle that touches every other noodle on the plate. It doesn't matter how many issues are out there, they can handle them all at the same time.

So there is a lesson to be learned here for the men and for the women. Women: I know in this day and age, we like to do everything ourselves. There are so many single mothers out there that when married they forget how to communicate with their husbands in a way that shows the man is the head of the family. Then they get a divorce and then she rides the roller coaster again!!

Women need to understand that it is important that you put the man before you for the order of the house to stay connected. The bible states this very clearly. God ordained that a wife would have tremendous power in her marriage, even as she willingly submits to her husband. *"To the woman he said, "I will greatly increase your pains in childbearing; with pain you will give birth to children. Your desire will be for your husband, and he will rule over you.""* Genesis 3:16. And *"Now I want you to realize that the head of every man is Christ, and the head of the woman is man, and the head of Christ is God.*" 1 Corinthians 11:3. So women, if you think your man is not living up to his duties then by all means lay it into him. He needs to understand things in layman's terms. (Or into a car manual description.)

Men: You need to understand that your wife is not trying to chastise you they are just trying to help you so that you won't look like a fool in front of your family. Thank them every chance you get. It's because of their wonderful insights that have made you the head of your family. And when making a decision, think before responding; think of what your wife will do if you make this decision. How would she handle it and what will be her response if you tell the children so. Also: Am I going to get into trouble if I make this decision instead of that one?

All of this should be running through your head while trying to make a decision. Too hard? Then remember this and it will help you along the way: Happy Wife, Happy Life. If your wife is happy then you will have a happy life. You might not be able to go to the golf game but you are happy. So men, just try and remember that you ARE the head of the family, but everything also must go through the woman for she can make you change your mind before YOU want to change it. Bear that in mind and follow those simple rules and you will be living like Kings. Or close to it. If your wife allows it. LOL!!!

Go forth and re-watch this movie. Which quote do YOU think can help you? And how will this quote help you?

*"The man is the head, but the woman is the neck. And she can turn the head anyway she wants."* – Lainie Kazan in *My Big Fat Greek Wedding*

# *November 17, 2:58pm*

## *Day 17*

It's 4:15am in the morning on a Saturday. A Saturday that I work, but it's just a four hour shift so it's not that bad. It seems that lately I just can't get any shut eye. Whatever I do, it just feels like time is slipping away from me if I close my eyes, and I don't want that to happen. There are so many things I want to do, to accomplish right here, right now and I know it just won't happen.

My body wants to take a break, but my brain keeps pushing it, telling it that it can't take a break, not for one minute. I have to keep pressing on; I have to keep fighting the time loss. When sleeping, my brain knows I should get this done, and it won't let me get the rest I need so badly. So many things going on at the same time it doesn't seem possible that I have any time to myself anymore.

Ever since I was little, I was fascinated by the way

watches worked. The way that the little gears inside one of those watches can just twirl around and keep time available for us. Amazing. Well, I'm also very attached to the way I spend my time on things, and it just seems like I don't have that much time to do anything anymore. When I was a child, it seemed like I had all the time in the world, my time was my adventure.

Each time I close my eyes, my brain comes up with something that I know I have to write down and I won't feel right if I don't. It might not even mean anything later, but my brain believes I should write it down fast. I don't think I mentioned this on my other days but whenever I write, I have to listen to music. I get that from my mother's side. I have to have music going whenever I'm thinking of something. When it was homework, I had Jazz going and, know what? I remembered what I was studying, and it helped me think.

Music usually lifts my spirits up and it also clears my mind. Mostly I listen to Jazz, Big Band, Classical music but I also listen to many other songs. Like right now; I'm listening to Kenny Chesney's *Soul of a Sailor*. I really enjoy that song. It's so much like me and my family. *"I can't be stilled, I can't be tied."* Who really can? When there is so much to see out there in the world and so little time to do it. Uh-oh. I don't believe it! I CAN'T believe it. I'm a Pirate!! HA-HA.

I actually think that many of the sailors are writers at heart. And those writers are sailors at heart. Look at each one for one sec. A Sailor wants to seek new life, new adventures and see the ocean blue and enjoy the crisp wisp of water on their face.

Writers are like that too…they seek new life and new adventures when they have learned how to write words on a tablet somewhere. They may not want to get sprayed with water every single day, but the sentiment of the ocean is the same. They both want the feel of the length of the ocean, the feeling of adventure. Many times it's just the sea, the blueness of the ocean and the idea that it's so far away from the mainland, like trouble and all the problems of the world cast their problems in your lap. No, with being away from the world, and having nothing but the sea take your troubles away, who could say no to that?

And the ocean is such a romantic getaway as well

as a fast getaway from troubles.  Every time you go out in the vastness of the sea, there's just something romantic about it.  Something that sparks your inner self that ignites like a spark plug in a Ferrari.  There is so much life out there to live, who can blame writers to turn into Pirates once in a while to enjoy that life?

Look at Ernest Hemingway?  What a wonderful and interesting writer and he left his life on the mainland and enjoyed himself out there in the vastness of the seas. He took that opportunity at what God gave us and he brought it to us through his writing.  His way of living, was the result of the sea, the result of living in Paradise and seeing what God really intended for their lives.

I honestly believe that Hawaii or even the Caribbean was the Garden of Eden itself, because of the beautiful views it gives you, but also the Magic in the islands.  The Magic of living; the Magic of seeing for the first time ever that you really have a life to live for and how spending your time with your family results in that life. The Islands show and prove to you what you are doing to your family; and the Magic of romance.

I have on my wall in my living room a print of a

painting drawn by none other than Claude Monet from 1908. It's a picture of what looks like the waters of Venice. It's got the gondola that you always see in those Italian movies. The kind that takes you around Italy and you can go right up to your hotel that overlooks the little channels.

It's got the nicest color blue I have ever seen. And the structures of the buildings! I just love it. I love sitting down on my couch and just looking at the painting like it's alive. I can literally hear the river cozying up to the boats as they pass by; I can hear the sounds of parties, the laughter of people having the time of their lives; I can see the lights twinkling in the moonlight up and down the Venie town. See the love just sparkling along the air. The place of families/lovers getting together and having nothing but joy in their hearts.

That's what I get out of the quote from a movie that will surprise you. The movie is *Die Hard* with Bruce Willis. Now what can something so sweet, so innocent, so lovely have to do with a gun-totting-motherfu****-that now has a machine gun Ho Ho Ho?!?!

Because there is one line that always sticks in my

head. After watching it the first time, I couldn't stop saying it to people. ***"Come out to the coast, we'll get together, have a few laughs.***" I LOVE that quote. It's so like what I am thinking all the time; what I see in that picture hanging on my wall.

The one thing most people like to do is go by the water. Either you are a man, woman or child, you always want to go near the shore. Whether it is the Pacific Coast, Atlantic, or even the Gulf of Mexico, you always want to be near the water.

And there is always something to do by the water. Take Florida for instance; wherever you go, you see restaurants after restaurants. You see bars after bars. It's the places to go and get together just to have fun. That's what anybody wants really. They really just want a place to hang out; to have a few laughs.

Families too, you know. Families love to get together, enjoy each other's company and before the week is over they plan on killing each other, so where's the beer?

Going to the coast clears so many people's minds, and people start feeling refreshed and when they get back to their busy stressed life, they can start anew and figure things out better.

So that's my wish to you reader. (Wow, I actually have someone reading my book. Oh wait, that's just Ma. Hi Ma!) Take your family out to any coast, your choice (choose Florida, it's SO much fun) get wet; be merry and please, for Bruce's sake, have a few laughs!

Go forth and re-watch this movie. Which quote do YOU think can help you? And how will this quote help you?

*"Come out to the coast, we'll get together, have a few laughs."* – Bruce Willis in *Die Hard*

# *November 18, 4:14pm*

## *Day 18*

When people tell you it's a lazy Sunday afternoon, I totally know what they mean by that! It's 4:14 pm, sun is shining, and I'm inside writing on my computer for today's quote. I'm eating Wesco Popcorn and watching *Castle*. Well, actually I have the main menu up and the music where the person is whistling is on.

I like listening to it and watching all the different clips from different episodes. It kind of gets my mind working and thinking of different things that could happen in my stories or in this case just looking at Nathan Fillion.

If I start watching any of the shows, I put the laptop down and just watch; forgetting that I have a contest to win and a book to finish. Darn you Nathan Fillion!! But, oh my GOD!! If you have not yet tried Wesco Popcorn, then my heart goes out to you! You don't know what great popcorn it is; I would even say it's better than the theater popcorn. You don't need to add any kind of butter to it, or any salt or whatever you people put on your popcorn, it's the best kind all by itself.

The only thing is I have nothing to drink. This time I have no Mountain Dew, I have no orange juice, nor do I have milk. Oh the horror!! The only thing I have is blah! water and, um, some packets of what looks like lemonade. I can't believe I don't have anything to drink! Wait; I just re-read that last line and did I just put down packets of lemonade? I'm saved. Let me be quick about opening a packet of lemonade.

So this is what my life has become, folks. I'm a sleeper by morning, librarian in the afternoon and a writer by nightfall. Wow, I am living the life. I'm all set for the New Year and am making a killing at it. People should be writing books about me instead of me writing a book for other people. If you look at my refrigerator right about now, you would see: eggs, mustard, and butter, two slices of ham left over from a sandwich and whip cream. That's right, I said Whip Cream, the kind you get in the can. (There are so many kinky scenarios going through your head right about now aren't there? What I could be doing with *Whip Cream* in my refrigerator, especially *two* cans? I'll let you enjoy this thought for a sec…okay, seconds up.)

And no, it's not what you think! I'm not that kinky and I don't have a boyfriend, so all those little theories just went right out the window. I love to eat Whip Cream right out of the can on days that I just can't seem to eat anything else. Some would say that this is an act of being a child, and that the person is psychologically disturbed and must be checked out. And you would be right.

Yes, I do sometimes act like a child, but there is nothing wrong with my head, really. I just don't like the idea of growing up too fast. I'd like to still be able to enjoy the little things in life and not have to look back and wish I could be a kid again.

When you are growing up you have those wishes and dreams. As a kid those dreams of becoming an astronaut, a police officer, firefighter, a doctor, or an actor was the highlight of their life. Some of those dreams come from watching movies, or listening to the stories from books or from families. Stories about adventures or about true life events just get the blood pumping. Many of those dreams turn into being a hero for us.

Heroes like Han Solo, Indiana Jones, James Bond, and Princess Diana. Or if you're like me, then it would be a comic book hero. When I was a kid I really enjoyed reading and that included tons of books from kid versions to adult versions and then it evolved into comic books. Batman, Superman, Green Lantern, The Avengers. When you're a kid, you dream of going to different places, to different worlds to become something great like your heroes, whoever they are. You start out small: you start watching the shows, you ask for the books, for the toys of your favorite hero. Then you start getting big: you buy the movies; you go to the comic-cons and start collecting the books or comics. Then it gets expensive whereas you start in with the making of your very own costume. Then finally you see about meeting that hero. For those of you who are snickering in the back, yes I am a huge GEEK!!! I am a Batman/Avengers fan. Batman because he had billions of dollars and the coolest gadgets; The Avengers because they have a Hulk and will avenge anyone who will TRY and destroy their world!

Then I got to thinking about when I was a kid, who was my hero? Of course it was my mother. I think I have already established that through my other quotes that my mother has always been and will always be my hero.

She stood by me through everything; she protected me during the good times, and through the bad times. She let me dream of anything I wanted to be and let me pursue it to a point. She never pushed me into anything I didn't want to do, and she pushed me into things that I wanted to do. She always gave me encouragement and love when times got bad. I don't know how she always knows I need it, but she does. And that ladies and gents is my hero.

But I guess I am entitled to one more hero aren't I? I bet you're wondering who it is? A teacher, an officer of the law, or is it a neighbor? Neither.

His name is John-Boy Walton. Everything I learned about writing I learned from watching him when I was a kid. Every morning before I had to go to school it was Star Trek or The Walton's, whichever comes on first and there I am watching John-Boy writing about his family and days of his life and I'm like, that's what I want to do. Just write about people and share it with the world. To be able to put your life in words and for it be interesting enough for others to read it. A little embarrassment time for me: I use to write my name as John-Boy. I wanted to be just like him in every way. Come on folks, I was 4. I couldn't write a full sentence but I sure was making line after line of "stuff".

Another thing that I really enjoyed about the The Walton's were the stories of how the families lived through the depression and such but also the back story of how John-Boy grew up as a country boy and had dreams of going to New York to become a writer and was worried if he would lose who he was. His thinking about himself was always "I'm just a country boy. I don't think I can make it in the big world." And then he proved them all wrong.

It's because of his "country boyisms" that actually got him through the world. Because he didn't lose who he was, where he came from, he actually made it through the world with the world loving him. That takes a lot of courage to stay true to who you are and not falter to what the world wants you to be.

I see that all the time while working at the library. I see really nice, polite kids and when they get into High School or into the world, they are totally "like the world"! Mean, self-centered, selfish bunch of teenagers this world has ever seen and that's because they lost who they were. They forgot where they came from and that frightens them. So they try to fit into the world and they let the world make a new ID for them.

Not a nice fitting way to make it into the world, but if one doesn't keep their "birth" place with them, if they try to forget who they are inside, then that is what they will become. They will always have this empty feeling in their heart, the emptiness of "where did I come from" to "where am I going".

That's the big aspect in people's lives: Where they are going. In life, we are always looking forward; where we are headed and why are we here. We can't move on till we know that answer.

To find that answer? Look to where you started it all!! Where you came from really coats who you are and who you will become. Kind of deep I know, but it's the truth. If you look at society today, you can tell it's the truth. Many kids that grew up on the bad side of the tracks usually continue with that style of life: the thug life! That's where they were born, that's what they grew up with and are not likely to change.

But sometimes, there are a few people that come out of the thug life and try to make a name for themselves because of the place they were born in, the place where they all grew up and saw all there was to see. They actually move on and make a change in their life, always remembering where they came from so they don't have to go back to that lifestyle!

Like John-Boy, there are many who remember their birth place as a wonderful time to grow up, and they make their future a wonderful place as well. It's not so much what other people do to help you along the way; it's what YOU make out of it. When you see the world around you as a wonderful learning experience you will most likely have that in your own home wherever you end up.

If you live in a world where there is turmoil, hatred and unconsciousness from drugs or alcohol, you will probably grow up to be sucked into all of that or you have the CHOICE to make up your own future wherever you want it, and can have that wonderful life of good choices. It all takes effort to actually make a name for yourself in your own life and not what others want your life to be. But never forget where you came from. It's what drives you to who you are today.

And as always, there is a quote that helps you remember or think more on what I'm talking about. This quote is from a newer movie that just came out and at first I didn't think I was going to use it, because who is going to say this to themselves and think about where they came from and how they can overcome anything because of their home town?

But I started hearing people really liking this quote, smile each time they hear it from the trailers and it just got me thinking this would be a good one.

The quote is said by Chris Evans from his hit *Captain America*: ***"I'm just a kid from Brooklyn."*** Not a whole lot of references in the movie address this quote, but it is said periodically in the movie so it must mean something to the writers.

To me, Captain America is so humble about himself, that he won't take all the credit of WHY they choose him for this experiment, that he didn't do anything astounding to be remembered by all.

He's just a kid from Brooklyn. But because he kept himself so humble through all the turmoil that had happened to him, and all the hatred towards him and his country, he keeps that homage memory of his time in Brooklyn. He remembers the time he got beaten up in different alleys. That made him stronger and made him stand up to his beliefs. He remembers his time with his friend: that made him complete, to know that he has a friend that doesn't criticize the things he does. And Brooklyn has always been known for people "talking back" to whoever is criticizing them so he knows how to stand up on his own two feet with words as well as his fists.

Also in Brooklyn the people learned the hard way to stand up for others as well as your own back. They look out for their families, and their friends. He understands the importance of friends and allies because of Brooklyn and he will remember that all the days of his life.

So what will you remember? What will you bring forth with you as you grow older? When you move, will you keep those memories of where you were when you were young? Will you let your past shape your future or turn it around so it will benefit you and your family?

If you only remember the bad, will you KEEP the bad inside you, or will you overcome that and become who YOU want to be?

Choices, choices. It takes Effort to become who or what you will become, there will be hardships. But don't forget the past. Some of the time you do have to let go to actually move on, but don't ever forget. Your background makes you who you are: join with it or overcome it.

Go forth and re-watch this movie. Which quote do YOU think can help you? And how will this quote help you?

*"I'm just a kid from Brooklyn"* – Chris Evans in *Captain America*

# *November 19, 12:31pm*

## *Day 19*

As I sit in the nearest coffee shop, I see something that just astounds me. Not only is there such a thing as a coffee shop (it's actually Starbucks, but let's go with the flow here), and that there are tons of people ranging from 18-45 years of age. Even more interesting, it's like in all those movies: they are all either reading, writing or dealing some sort of business on their smart-phone, iPad or laptop.

It just astounds me how far my generation has gotten. Who knew that when Gates and Jobs build that computer in their garage that they were building an Enterprise!! It's amazing to see these people hunched over their devices like their lives depend on them. In other words, that's true. In a way...I mean, where are we without the technology that is available to us right now? What would our world be like? We wouldn't have the luxury of calling our families who live across the world and be able to "see" them as well! We wouldn't be able to make business deals at home for the company building in Japan!

Look at the different games that need the internet, the Wi-Fi. We wouldn't have the fun, the competition of the strategic gaming that we have today. Imagine using a pen and paper to do accounting. It was done before, but look how simple it is to use now! What if you lived 10 miles from your work? Do you honestly see yourself "walking" 10 miles to work? (And I'm talking to the people that actually depend on their cars not the walking/running people, Save the Planet types. Nothing wrong with that, but it doesn't prove my point.)

And how about things that keep us entertained, like *Movies*! That is what this book is all about. About how movies help sharpen our lives, help us through tough times. When we see other people go through it, we see in our minds "Yes, I can get through this. If Tom Hanks can handle being on his own for years on an island with nobody but *Wilson* then I think I can handle my boss for the next few days."

There are a lot of certain types of technology that is used for making a movie, producing a movie and watching the movie. It used to be we had to go to Drive-Ins or watch on huge TV boxes with five inch screens.

Then it moved into flat screen TV's with enormous viewing; then to hand-held devices to watching them on your computer. Next we will have a device that is similar to a contact and when put in your eye, you get to watch a personal movie while walking to work! (As an accident prone person, I dread when that day comes!!) So technology has worked out real well for people in the entertainment world and business status.

But with all the times that people are on their devices or at work how are they going to find the love of their life? With so much time spent in front of the computer, when do these people find time to go to the clubs, go to a dating restaurant or be like Barney in *How I Met Your Mother* and try the Lemon Law? They don't.

There are so many people online right now and they should be out there looking for the right mate instead of killing the Ogre Guard Keeper in Infinity Blade Bloodline II (sorry, favorite game had to put it in here).

My generation is doomed in the reproducing of the next generation!!

But what if I told you that now it has come full circle and the technology we have today can help you find your soul mate? What would you say to that? You can finally find that mate through the internet!

I am not making this stuff up! There are now markets of web sites available to you for free or for a fair price. There's eHarmony; Match; Zoosk; Plenty of Fish; and plenty more! You can go online, fill out a profile, should be the truth; state things about you that you would normally say on your first date. A little bit of background on your life, on your family and your Zodiac sign and just let the computer crunch a few numbers and you have you a match in less than 5 minutes. Amazing! Can't go wrong with that! (Okay, so I've tried a few of those sites myself. STOP JUDGING ME!! I'm a very busy girl and I hardly have a social life that's not with my parents or the library ladies. I've tried, no luck just yet, but I'm still trying. There I said it. Let's move on.)

It seems like it all just started a few years back. It feels like it's just becoming a new thing when in fact it was used back in 1940. It wasn't exactly email, chat rooms; more like letters. Mail, it was called mail back then. Man wrote a letter to an ad in the paper and got a response from a woman. Not knowing who she was, fell madly in love with her; while disliking a woman that he works with not realizing the woman he despises is also the woman he loves.

Sounds familiar? Well it should be. One of James Stewart's big hits, *The Shop Around the Corner*. Great movie. Shows that, yes, you can love someone without really meeting them. Not the movie for today, but a movie just like it set for our time-frame.

A movie made in '98, that deals with computers and love "letters" via email. Going to the post office to see your letter is not "cool" anymore. *You've got mail* are much more powerful words and an easy open liner. Of course in this case, that's the name of the movie for today, and the line. ***You've Got Mail*** are some powerful words if you're looking for someone to spend your life with.

So many movies evolve around the idea of love and the admiration between the main characters. Interesting enough this movie has used the technology as the middle man between the two characters. In this day and age, technology plays so much in our lives we don't even notice it. The way writers write: through computers or using apps on their iPads (Like I do); the way police officers find suspects: using computers to track their whereabouts; researcher's searching past history; and then people started using technology to find their soul mates.

Weird right? I mean who does that? Who trusts their love on some type of machine that can crunch a few numbers and say "Here you go your soul mate. Let's talk"? Oh wait...I do!! LOL!

There are so many different ways to find love these days so why not try it out?! Beforehand there were different ways of finding true love...family introducing the two of you, friend of a friend knows a guy, the old bar trick. Now, it's "emailing" each other. A guy in New York goes online, and finds the love of his life living in California. Now what are the chances that they would have met in a bar across town; or met in the subway on the way to work? Zip, nada. The only way?

Through the internet.

I guess that's why this movie has been a huge hit with a lot of people. So many couple's stories start with "We met in some chat room..." and many of them succeed more than those that meet at a bar. Now I'm not saying that's how ALL people should meet, but it's a great start. For one, it helps you see who YOU really are. Taking those tests for the online machine to crunch up the numbers really asks personal and insightful questions that you yourself never thought of asking or telling someone on your first date. Those tests really make you look deep inside you and show you who you're really looking for instead of the usual: Tall, dark and handsome.

That will always be on the list of things to look for in "your" man, but there are many other aspects to be looking for. And the online dating helps you outreach your parameters.

I'm not saying that you should trust every male user online, (there are some really creepy guys out there just looking for a one-night stand).

Just look at yourself and the results that you come up

with and you could find your guy in no time. Once you establish who YOU really are, looking for Mr. Right just became a whole lot easier.

Go forth and re-watch this movie. Which quote do YOU think can help you? And how will this quote help you?

*"You've Got Mail."* Tom Hanks in *You've Got Mail*

# *November 20, 8:15am*

## *Day 20*

I'm having the time of my life right about now. I am over half way through my book here. I'm getting ideas after ideas about what to write these days. So many new quotes to sift through, to think "does this quote really help out my life"?

I'm constantly thinking while I'm writing how this quote will help me in making my life better than it already is. I think of new ways to give me a headache and this is it. There are so many movies to choose from and trying to think of them the night beforehand so that I am ready for tomorrow's task is not an easy job. It's actually really hard.

But, back to me having the time of my life right now. It's not so easy having the time of my life when things are so wrong in America, but I'm doing it. I'm having a great time. I'm watching my favorite show Firefly; I'm talking to friends on Tumblr; and I have the whole day to myself for it is Sunday. I don't have to go to work; my parents are taking the day off and waiting to watch Football. The game that I want to see is at 6:00 so I have like how many hours to kill here? Like a lot.

I'm so glad that I have so many hours to work on my book because I'm tired from not sleeping. I'm hungry and all I have is tuna fish sandwiches; I have no toilet paper; and I need Mountain Dew but I'm fresh out of it!!! Oh yea, I'm having the time of my life alright!!! Time for having a HEADACHE!!! Excuse my French for saying this but the world can be one shi-double-hockey-sticks-y place!!!

People arguing with others over nothing; people crying and weeping on your shoulder thinking that you can make the pain go away and when that pain doesn't go away, they blame you for everything and there goes your friendship!!! And that's just on Tumblr!!! Think of what I will find out when I check my Facebook and Twitter accounts.

Okay...I'm going to take a little timeout here and I'm going to explain a little bit about Social Networking, just for those that are reading this that have NO IDEA what I'm talking about.

Pretty much everybody has heard of Facebook. A young Harvard student got drunk one night; got angry with his not-girlfriend; decided to make this page where everybody knows everybody that can comment on everybody; and made millions of dollars. Kids love it. Parents are skeptical about it. Well, you get the idea of Facebook.

Twitter: you tweet about your interesting exciting life in 140 characters or less!! Heck, you can even fall in love with someone in 140 characters or less. (If you have not read *Goodnight Tweetheart* by: Teresa Medeiros then you are missing out.) And it's also a great place to see what your favorite stars are doing at that precise moment in 140 characters or less. As you can see I am stressing the 140 characters or fewer things BECAUSE THAT IS ALL YOU GET TO SAY!!! And as you can see I'm a big talker, so that kind of puts a cramp in my style!! But now on to Tumblr.

Tumblr is the place where anyone can go online and talk/chat/show their pictures/show their favorite videos, and show your favorite trends without having to share your real name.  Heck, I'm '*Coffee2House0*' and blog about things that I would not put in my Facebook page which has my real name on it.  I love Tumblr.  I have friends all over the place: London/Florida/California/Oregon/Canada …many more.  It's fantastic.  There is no limit, and I can have serious fun.  I actually get in trouble sometimes at work because I'm on there so many times.

Once I really embarrassed myself:  I was at work (the library for you probies) and there weren't a lot of people there so I indulged myself on Tumblr ad was watching the *Castle* trends, just reading a post, when the phone rang.  Normally I say, "Shelby Library, this is Kelsey."  Nope.  "Shelby Library this is Castle."  C A N Y O U BELIEVE THAT?!?!?!?!  I covered myself pretty good so I don't think the person on the line heard me, but my co-workers did!!  Man, talk about embarrassment.  But Tumblr is still fun.

What does this little biography have to do with my

next quote?  Well, it's because of Tumblr that my day today is not turning out to be a great one.  Post after post I see kids my age and a little bit younger are heartbroken. It's from a bad break up, school is too hard or they are having problems at home.  Cry after cry; tear after tear, and I'm trying to figure out how to help them and trying to dissect what they are going through.

It's a losing battle but it really sucks you into their chaos.  It's like having your own Soap Opera at your fingertips!  My parents and friends at the library see this and they wonder, why not just ditch Tumblr?  Why put yourself into their hands and their messed up lives?

Why?  It's kind of hard to explain but I'll try.  I like to help people.  This book ought to tell you that:  I'm trying to help YOU in YOUR own life.  Anyway…I see these people on Tumblr and their issues and I want to help them.  Whether it is with words/videos or just plain pictures, whatever will do the trick, I'm posting it.

Pictures speak a thousand words, and on Tumblr, it really matters to people.  But man!  It gets kind of…what word am I thinking of…sad?…no…teary-eyed?…no…traumatizing?  Yea…that's it.  Traumatizing to see so many people going through the same old things and wondering how to get through it with a smile on their face.

Interesting enough, I find myself wrapped into the whole ordeal and I'm up till 3 in the morning trying to talk it over with three different people going through the same stuff.

One night I had enough! I couldn't take it anymore. Many of the things that they are crying over were stupid things. They couldn't get their phones working so they start throwing crap around on the internet; or their boyfriends/girlfriends left them hanging and they were wanting to commit suicide.

I know people often say what they don't mean, but they kept posting pictures of death or of people cutting themselves and they were talking about maybe doing it themselves.

I was like, seriously? You're going to go through all of this crying for some guy that can't see that what he's got is something great, and you are really going to scream and whine all over your blog over something that stupid? You idiot! Cry for a while…eat some ice cream…and move on. Get through all of this nonsense about cutting yourself, and letting your life go for some idiot.

And will you stop crying!!!!

Many of them tell me it's none of my business; they ask me what's wrong with me? Many of them say go to…wait! That's wildly inappropriate, so I can't say that here! But many of them ask me, how can they get through it without crying so much? What do I do, they ask me.

What do I do? Well, I think about how stupid the boy would be for letting me go; or how wrong the taxes are for taking all of my money, or how my car can be so stupid sometimes that I just want to break down and cry myself.

So how do I get through life without bawling my eyes out? Easy. I think of this line from a famous movie and I get through it. Wanna know which line it is?

*"Are you crying? ARE YOU CRYING? There's no crying! THERE'S NO CRYING IN BASEBALL!"* It's from *A league of Their Own* starring Tom Hanks.

A great movie and this is one of my favorite lines.

You are probably thinking, how can this line help me not to cry? Well, try saying this exactly as Tom Hanks did in front of a mirror and you will see yourself cracking up over it.

The line is hilarious; the look he gives her is just phenomenal, you just can't stop yourself from laughing. It brightens my day when I say this line and it's so true. In baseball you don't have any *TIME* to be crying on the field. You need to be getting off the field, or finish the inning.

One time I was playing softball (and many of you who know about softball, they are not soft and they are HUGE!!!) and I was the third baseman. The batter hit the ball hard and it went sailing towards my way. I knew I had it so I went into my stance and got ready to catch the ball. Well I guess I misjudged where the ball was going and it hit the tip of my glove and bounced up and *SMACKED!* me right in the chest. It hurt like hell, let me tell you!!

I got the ball and I threw it to first base and luckily enough got the runner out! But we still had one more out to go so I waited till our inning was over. I had to wait through two more batters and my chest was throbbing something fierce but I still covered third base and hung in there.

After our inning was over I went into the dugout, grabbed my chest and huddled on the bench till someone came over with ice. That's when I started crying. After that my chest was bruised all over but the main point is, I didn't cry during the game for there is NO CRYING IN BASEBALL!!

So how can something like this line help you out in the real world even though you're not in baseball? Easy…just apply it to whatever you're doing in life and when something starts pinning you down and you want to scream, say this line. Either say it silently in your head or go into the bathroom, close the stall and scream this line at the top of your lungs *"Are you crying?  ARE YOU CRYING?  There's no crying IN BASEBALL!!!!"*

You will definitely see yourself stop slamming your head against the wall trying to figure things out and you will actually see the answer flash before your very eyes on how to handle the situation.

Tom Hanks probably didn't realize how much this quote would help people out all over the world. Or how much it helped me reach these kids that are going through all this "turmoil" in their life on Tumblr.

So folks that are reading this: Your boss is yelling at you for something that you clearly had nothing to do with but have to take it …There is no crying in baseball. Girls: your boyfriend is leaving you because of something stupid that happened between you, don't start thinking that your life is over and do not contemplate suicide…There's no crying in baseball. You've missed the deadline for your bills…There's no crying in baseball!!!

Just get over yourself, buck up and move on. Get the stuff done for your boss and do extra work on it so he will stop yelling at you; girls, there are over 5 billion men in the world, so no rush. Missed a deadline on your bills? Who hasn't? Just call them up, explain and send them a check when you can.

Just remember…THERE'S NO CRYING IN BASEBALL!!! Go forth and re-watch this movie. Which quote do YOU think can help you? And how will this quote help you?

*"Are you crying?  ARE YOU CRYING?  There's no crying!  THERE'S NO CRYING IN BASEBALL!"*

– Tom Hanks in *A League of Their Own*

# *November 21, 7:50 pm*

## *Day 21*

Life is unique…it's never the same.  There are days where nothing is going your way and other days it's just the way you like it!  Each day will present itself with new troubles; new adventures that you must partake in to achieve your life span.

Life is surprising…you never know what you will receive in your own Mushroom Kingdom.  You never know if you will have to save a Princess from a terrible Turtle of some kind.

Life is…interesting.  Life will give you room enough to roam around in but then it will suck you bone dry of everything you own.  You can be free one minute but then in shackles in another.  Quite literally life can be very unexpected.  Everything we do in our lifetime has a huge effect on the world. Doesn't' matter if we stay in small towns, which shows you how one person can change the entire town, or if we stay in a big city and it takes tens of thousands of people to change the city.

People have a way of surprising people. Living in a small town? Not thinking you can do anything that would change the world? Think again. Living in a huge city? Thinking that one tiny person in a hundreds and thousands population couldn't possibly change the outlook for that city? Whatever you do, however you do it, it will affect the people in towns and cities. It could do great things, not only to you, but to the world.

You never know what people will do with information that could mean so little to us but have a huge impact on the world. And you don't have to be Bill Gates to change the world; nor do you have to be a millionaire to change people's lives for the better. Money really doesn't need to play an important role in trying to help someone.

You just need to know what to say, and how to say it and realize your actions speak louder than your words. You just need to be compassionate towards those that need help. Life is something to live for. Even though life will throw you to the darkest pit of hell you could ever imagine, there was a purpose laid out for you there. You are thrown to that pit, either it is New York, Chicago, Las Vegas or Lost Springs, Wyoming, there was a purpose for YOU to be there.

Either it's to help people in need or the way things are set for people's lives. But there is always a reason for us to be where we are or where we are going. Even if you aren't Bill Gates or Donald Trump, you have that responsibility to do something that can change the course of the future for all.

To sum this all up so that everybody can understand, I will refer to that movie favorite Lord *of the Rings: Fellowship of the Ring* with "***Even the smallest person can change the course of the future***."

I know I know. I actually went there. What can I say, I'm a librarian and I'm a geek. Wonderful combination isn't it MEN???? This excerpt is so very true. We all as human beings have it etched into our DNA that if you want to make it in this world you have to do something that keeps this world turning. Whether it be donations, and I mean HUGE donations; to third world countries; saving the children through songs or money and you must have power to actually make things possible, to change the course of the future for all.

And that's all movies and rich men telling us puny little townies and nobodies that we can't "help" make the world turn around.

People are always watching on the news how George Clooney is helping another family that is living through turmoil in Africa; how Brad Pitt and Angelina Jolie adopted another child from a poverty life from another country. That's what the news cares about.

Not about Joe the Plummer donating his time and his brains on fixing the pipes in a hotel, or a neighborhood. You don't hear how Susie made 53 quilts and donated them to the entire local Fireman's Fund and Susie never asked for a dime.

Where's the news about that? That's what happened to our world. That's why nobody lifts a finger to help their neighbors out anymore. They aren't getting the recognition for their help. Why help someone when you don't get credit for it? And how is something as puny as making a bunch of quilts that will keep children warm gonna affect the future? How can ONE person help keep the world turning?

By using the "E" word. That's what my father always said. (For those of you who have been reading this for a while you have met my mother, you have met my brother, now it's time to meet my dad. For those who just picked this book up: Welcome.)

My father is a man of a lot of words. He knows what to say, how to say it and when the right time it is to say it. He is a loving Christian man that follows the Word of the Lord. He also has "been there and done that." He knows the people of the town for he grew up with this small town that I live in now.

He knows who will help me in certain situations and he knows who I should NOT go to in certain situations. To me, he's like John Walton from the *Walton's* show. If someone has a problem, they turn to him; if they need help in a situation, they turn to him. If they just want to sit and chat over a cup of coffee and a donut, they turn to him. He's just the kind of guy you can go to for help, and help you will receive.

That's what I learned from him. I learned that if someone needs help, help them the best that YOU can, and if you see you're just helping a lost cause, then sorry but I won't be able to help you until you help yourself.

But my father always taught me if you need to do something, put all your Effort into it. That's where the "E" word comes in. "Oh they didn't want to do this so I ended up doing it." My dad's response? "It's all about the "E" word Kelsey. And they don't have it." My dad would actually say it to their face sometimes if the timing was right.

So if you're thinking that you are too puny to help others or too small to help keep the world go round, I command you to STOP!!!! *__Even the smallest person can change the course of the future.__* Look at Frodo. Look at what he did and how he accomplished something that tall, dark handsome men couldn't do.

Do you think Aragon could willingly do what Frodo did? Maybe, but he wouldn't have been able to handle Gollum with his twisted mind. Frodo did. Frodo had that heart of a Hobbit where he looked to Gollum for help. Anyone else besides Gandalf would probably have killed Gollum, on the first day.

So Frodo had to do all these amazing things to get to Mount Doom and throw away what almost consumed him. He even had a friend help him out who was as small as he.

To answer all your questions about life? Yes. Even YOU can change the course of the future; YOU can change the flow of normality in life; YOU could change a small town's views on things that would make the town grow.

Don't limit yourself because of your size; color; how much schooling you have or don't have. You can do anything you want but you have to be able to give all your "E" word-all your effort- into doing what you want. Nobody is going to give you all the answers to the world's problems and nobody is going to say "Oh, you're hurting? Okay. You get a free pass to go through this world. No more troubles for you, okay?"

Come on people!!! Wake up. There are no free passes for this world, there are no manuals that you can take home and study. You have to learn as you go, and make the best of things. Doesn't matter if you are poor;

rich; crippled; lame; speech impaired; too tall; too short; have Tourette's, or just ordinary.

YOU are able to figure out what God has in store for you, and it's nothing that you aren't capable of accomplishing. And yes, whatever your gifts are, whatever you are meant to do will change the course of the future. It will actually have an impact on people's lives in the future.

We talked about Frodo and what he did in the movie *Lord of the Rings*. Think of the actors and actresses that played our favorite characters out of that movie. Think they changed the course of the future for us all? Think they impacted people's lives with their quotes, their acting? Yes they did. They showed the people whole new worlds that even if it is fantasy, it is something we can strive for. A world with possibilities that would make a grown man strives for. Something we have been dreaming about and now have the chance to see it come to life before our very eyes has definitely changed the aspect of people's lives.

*The Lord of the Rings* will always be known as a classic movie of our generation; a movie that will stand out above all others that speaks about friendship, love, humbleness, how to be strong, and what it really means to fight for something that could kill you and your friends but still taking care of what needs to be done.

It's all about the "E" word. The effort to actually do something that will get the job done. And when you get the job done right, it will change your outlook on life. For you, your family and for the rest of world's future. Just watch how Frodo uses the "E" word in the three most fabulous movies ever made!

Go forth and re-watch this movie. Which quote do YOU think can help you? And how will this quote help you?

*"Even the smallest person can change the course of the future*."-Cate Blanchett in *Lord of the Rings: Fellowship of the Ring*

# *November 22, 2:24pm*

## *Day 22*

Remember that famous quote that mother used to say? "That may be an explanation but it is not an excuse?" This was usually said in the teenage years, but I'm pretty sure every mother has said this once or twice to their children.

Lot of people these days' are always trying to explain their actions, sometimes going on forever explaining why they did what they did. Even though it was wrong, they still feel the need to explain their actions.

Why? Because nobody wants to take the blame and just move on, they want to make sure that EVERYBODY knows that it wasn't their fault, even though it really was. It's like nowadays kids don't want to take responsibility for their actions and will spend an hour arguing about something they know they did wrong trying to get themselves out of trouble, but just wasting their time and others.

It doesn't even make sense if you think about it. The only reason I am trying to tell you what you did wrong in something is so you will be able to do it right the next time. I don't need a whole novel on your explanation of why you did it; there is no excuse for your actions. You can't justify (which excuse really means) the wrongful actions that you decided on your own to take.

It used to really bother me. From time to time I would find myself almost breaking and yelling at the person and just say, I don't care why you did it, try not doing it again! What you did was wrong and I don't have time to explain why it was wrong.

I guess people think that if they explain themselves into a novel then the blame will be lifted off them and they won't get into too much trouble. In my eyes they are still in the wrong and it's their fault for the results. But, you're just too tired to argue with them so you just finally give up and in the end they win.

I know one person, when told he did something wrong, boom, he starts explaining himself: why he did this, why he did that and totally tries to get the blame off of him. And yet everybody SAW him do this, they KNEW it was him. And nobody cares WHY he did it; he did it, so he should fix the problem.

But oh ho no…he has to tell you WHY he did it this way and when you try and tell him that way was actually wrong, he just cuts you right off and starts raising his voice over yours and proceeds to  everyone why he did it the way he did.

It's absolutely mind-boggling. Just take the blame, fix the problem, and let's all go merrily on our way. But how do you tell that person without totally embarrassing him and yourself? How do you get him to shut up?

Well, I found the perfect quote that can be said and it will totally shut the person up. Mostly because it takes them by surprise that I would even say this word, but also it takes them back a bit.

"*Frankly, my dear, I don't give a damn*," said by dashing Clark Gable to the lovely Vivien Leigh in *Gone with the Wind*. It's such a wonderful movie, but a long one at that. It's hard to follow if you don't watch from the beginning. But this one quote from this movie really has helped me out in a lot of ways.

How? Simple. When someone starts in on that "It wasn't my fault; this is the reason for it" I simply look at them, make them hush up a moment, and simply state the quote. "Frankly, my dear, I don't give a damn. Now, just go about your business and do the job right. This is how you do it...."

"Kind of mean" is probably going through your head right about now isn't it? How can a simple Christian woman say this, you're thinking? Easy. I'm so sick and tired of people not taking the responsibility of their own actions and trying to weasel their way out of it. To me that's a coward's way out. And trust me, when I say whomever is doing this is a coward, I'm not just talking about YOU. I'm also talking about ME as well as YOU.

You see folks, we all are not perfect. If there were Perfect Police Patrols, all 7 billion people will be in jail cells right now. Nobody is perfect, and I ain't either! I've done some things in my life that I know wasn't the perfect choice, but I lived with it. I didn't try and stick the blame on somebody else. I took it, and went on with my life.

So when someone starts giving me a hard time about a situation like that, I simply say this line and walk away. Yes, they will probably get mad at me. Yes, they might be a little pissed at me, but you know what? They do their job. They finally bite their tongue, they see from that one line that I mean business and it's of no use talking to me about it. They realize that I don't care for the whole drama queen or king bull scene.

That's mostly what it all is. Just drama. They want to have the excitement of blowing everything out of proportion because they either seek attention, they have some type of emotional dysfunction or they are trying to make life difficult for everyone around them.
And everything in their lives is a disaster that's more horrible than Hurricane Katrina so you better listen if you know what's good for you!!

These people need to realize that nobody cares. We don't care about your problems for we have problems of our own. We don't want a whole explanation of why you feel like you need to ruin people's lives with your bull.

And there is no way of changing a drama queen or king. You can't explain to one why what they do is wrong and hurtful to others. They know what they're doing is wrong but they do it anyway. Why? I seriously don't know. The human brain is a mysterious thing and I don't have quite all the answers for ya.

But I can tell you not to get bogged down by this. You shouldn't have to worry about their bull, just worry about you and yours. Take care of yourself before you start worrying about other people. How to get away from all of that bull? Just repeat the line Clark Cable tried to tell Vivien Leigh: *"**Frankly, my dear, I don't give a damn**.*" Try that sometime. See if it works for you.

Go forth and re-watch this movie. Which quote do YOU think can help you? And how will this quote help you?

*"**Frankly, my dear, I don't give a damn**"* – Clark Gable in *Gone with the Wind*

# *November 23, 5:15pm*

## *Day 23*

Have you noticed how many of these quotes I can make work for our generation, in our time frame so to speak? Kind of interesting. Quotes that were made in the '60s, '50s and even in the late '40s can still be applied to our time frame. And it really does help us. We are doing something in our lives that we have to contemplate whether or not this is a good idea, and we recall a quote, an excerpt from a film, and just that one line makes us smile and forget all the troubles in the world.

We recall that scene and it makes us smile because either we are thinking of the scene from the movie or what we were doing at the time we were watching that movie.

You could have been with your family at the time, enjoying each other's company or with a boyfriend or girlfriend and that event makes you smile in the present. Movies have a funny way of doing that to one's mind. Makes you remember the good times you had and have.

Some movies make you think of the double meaning behind the quote. Some movies make you see things that are happening in your world that you have never seen before. It makes all the nightmares come true, it makes all the fantasies come to life. Movies nowadays are making us see what the world has to offer and what the consequences will be like if we choose wrong.

But many don't realize that movies have always been like that. They are also a great device to get families back to talking and back to enjoying each other's company. Long ago families were eating meals together, spending time with each other and were actually doing family things. Nowadays it takes a huge catastrophe in the family for everyone to get together.

That's why I'm hoping that this book will help family members to realize what movies can do for not just yourself but for your family as well. To help build that bond that ties you all together and that never lets go.

There used to be a time when it didn't have to take a

movie to get the family together. To have them do things together, to participate in each other's conversations. People used to talk to one another. Used to be able to communicate freely with one another and somehow that got lost through the years.

Some were able to sit, drink a brew and listened to their fellow neighbor's problems, what's happening in town, and what's going on in their families. Now everybody is so busy they don't have time to just sit and listen to one another. I should actually take that back....everybody is so busy that they WON'T take time to just sit and listen....yeah, that about sums it all up.

Everyone is Twittering, using Facebook or using Tumblr where the whole world now knows what's going on with your life but your own family doesn't? Something's wrong here! We are forgetting how to carry on a conversation that doesn't involve LOL, WTF, OMG, PLOS, and many other texting terms.

It's very distracting and you don't learn anything about your family. We also don't pay enough attention to what the other person is talking about and we get lost in the conversation. When a word is said in this day and age, that one word could have three different meanings and it makes it hard to have a conversation when one person is thinking the word means this when it actually means that!

Our conversations would be like…would be like…Abbot and Costello's ***Who's on First?*** speech! Everyone knows which speech I'm talking about right?

**Costello:** What's the guy's name on first base?

**Abbott:** What's the guy's name on second base?

**Costello:** I'm not asking you who's on second.

**Abbott:** Who's on first?

**Costello:** I don't know.

**Abbott:** He's on third - we're not talkin' about him. Remember that skit? I am always cracking up about this skit. The way Costello is so innocent n what is going on, and Abbott is trying to tell him Who is On First, but gets frustrated that Costello doesn't understand him and it could go on forever.

But if you take a close look at what takes place in this skit, you will notice how much it actually represents this new Generation!! Kids these days don't know how to communicate with each other. Young parents don't know how to talk to one another, to have a conversation with each other to tell their other half how much they care for them.

Then they get into an argument over something so small and they don't get anything resolved and end up getting into a divorce all because they don't know how to communicate with each other.

Now for me...I love communication. I love conversations that take time to explain what one is feeling for the other. Let me explain...if one is in love with another, and that one is feeling some type of emotional feeling but keeps it inside, the other will think something is up and whenever we mortal human beings think something is up with their other, then it usually must mean something bad has happened and nobody wants to talk about it and it just builds up to this tension that is never released.

Me...I would sit down and actually talk to my boyfriend/husband/friend whatever the case may be, I would actually sit down and talk about my feelings, what I don't feel right about, or how much I love them. I'd literally tell them what I'm thinking right then and there and how I feel about it. I don't wait till the other starts asking questions, or starts getting mad. I talk to them right then and there (or wait till we get home) and it's resolved. Everyone is explaining themselves what is going on and nobody is left in the dark.

And I truly believe that is why there are so many divorces in this era. They are not taking the time to reach out and "explain" themselves or their feelings. They are so scared of what those feelings might mean to the other person so but why try right?

Wrong. I had to intervene for a couple once. It was family members so I won't mention any names but they just could not communicate with themselves if their lives depended on it. The husband came over and just poured out his heart. He needed someone to yell at, to cry to and I just happened to be there to listen. I let him finish his foaming at the mouth routine and when he was done, I let him have it.

See that's another key point: Let the person have their time of release. They have been holding on to whatever they are feeling, and if someone keeps interrupting them it just builds up more. So one of the things I try to do is let them have their time to just let it rip. Have them scream if they want to, let them speak their mind and what's eating at them. They will get tired soon and won't have anything else to say and that will give YOU enough time to process what they were saying to you and then help them out. First by saying I hear you, I understand what you were saying.

You ranted for (however many minutes or hours) so now it's my turn. Listen up. Then....let them have it. Don't hold back. Everyone else keeps holding back, this is not the time to think of their feelings at the moment. They need someone to actually tell them what the big picture is and fix it. And I did just that.

Then his wife walks in. The kids are at their grandparents so this was perfect timing, and I "kicked" him out of my house and dragged her into mine. See everything for some reason or another all of this was happening at my house. Once I dragged her into my house, I heard her side of the story. It was a little different but I got the gist of it. I tried telling her this is what she would need to do, and she kept crying "I tried this I tried that".

Well, that got me. I dragged my cousin back into the house and had them both sit. Facing each other. And I said, talk. I told them to say the same things that they said to me but to each other now.

And I left them. I think I walked down to the drugstore and got me some Mountain Dew, and when I came back an hour later, they were still talking. 3 hours later they came outside grinning from ear to ear. See what a little communication, the right kind, does to family members?

Instead of trying to say "Who's on First?" thinking that the other one knows that the man on first base is called Who, try saying that: The man on first's name is Who. That's him name, no joke. Everyone will be happy, the other person will understand and we can all go for a nice glass of Mountain Dew!

Of course we won't be getting any funny skits from it all, but life is not something for the television folks. Try having a conversation with each other. Even if it's a heavy one, if you two get to arguing, fine. JUST DO IT!!! Talk. Com-mu-ni-cation!!! It works, it really does. It takes time so try and figure out a way where you won't get interrupted and just talk. I think it would have helped Abbott's and Costello's relationship a bit, but then we wouldn't be having those laughs.

Go forth and re-watch this movie. Which quote do YOU think can help you? And how will this quote help you?

*"**Who's on first?**"* –Bud Abbott and Lou Costello in *The Naughty Nineties*

# *November 24, 8:15pm*

## *Day 24*

Gossip.  The definition of Gossip is:  one who chatters idly about others. Simple.  Another definition of Gossip is a Small Town, filled with tons and tons of women who like to "chatter idly about others."  In other words, women in small towns like to get together and talk about other people behind their backs.  And like to spread the word to other folks that are privy of such information.  When you live in a small town everyone knows someone that knows everything.

That's the secret of a small town.  You know everyone's business and you love it.  You love hearing how Susie hit Tommy on the playground; how Frank beat up Joe for looking at Frank's girl; and how Mrs. Smith is seeing Mr. Jones, and Mr. Smith doesn't know about it, unless for some reason he just happens to walk into Char's Beauty Parlor where all the ladies are cutting into it! Now that's entertainment, folks!

Truly, that's how it is in a small town. Don't believe me? Go to a place that has the population of 1500 (+ or − 100) and walk into a beauty parlor, or even the town's bakery. Sit down, read a newspaper, order some food and wait. Just wait. I guarantee you, in the next five minutes you will know everything and anything about what Susie did and why and how Carol found out from her friend of a friend of her sister. And you don't even know who Susie is.

Sort of reminds you of a movie, don't it? And it's not just the ladies…it's the men as well. Men don't gossip as much as the ladies but men are also held responsible for some rumors starting. Instead of the beauty parlor, it's the Bakery or the Town's Mechanic Shop. At any rate, if you live in a small town you will know everybody and everybody's business whether you want to or not.

Now I have that joy of living in a small town. And by joy I mean OMG!!! do I know everything about everybody! Not complaining here folks, just letting you know what's going on. In my small town, you can't keep secrets for there are no secrets. I know what happened last night at 11:31pm and I was asleep!!! Oh, but I heard about it the next morning. Sometimes it's a good thing, just in case I knew the person or if something happened that could result in some way affecting me in my lifetime that I need to be prepared for and I need to know about it.

But mostly, it's kind of fun to stick your nose in those places! We are very nosey human beings, and we want to be in each other's lives and not miss out on anything. Sometimes it's wrong, sometimes it helps. Hard to figure out which one is true, but that's life I guess.

I'm trying to remember which movie portrays this lovely town's gossipy women. It portrayed the gossip, the love, tragedy in families, coping through a loss with friends, but most important the gossip. I think it even took place in a Beauty Parlor as well. Now if only I could remember the name of that movie.

Was it: *I know what you did last summer*? No couldn't be that. It's a horror movie, and I don't watch horror movies. (*Chucky* was horror enough for me.)

There's gotta be a movie that fits the profile...AWHA!!!
I remember which movie it was.

When I mention gossip, you all are thinking of
women, right? Right. And where do women usually
hang out and spend the day just gossiping? At a beauty
parlor, right? Right. And the movie that brings them all
together is none other than that wonderful chick-flick
*Steel Magnolias*. A wonderful film that mothers should
share with their daughters before their daughters hit
puberty.

I love watching this movie with my mother. It's one
of those films that we can relate to and can talk about.
It's about a southern family that talks about everyday
things in life and while trying to have a family, the
daughter is dealing with diabetes, and it brings hardships
throughout the family but it doesn't stop them from
having a life. They try everything they can do to have a
normal life but sometimes that's not so easy with a small
town where everyone knows everything. Trust me, I
know.

How can something like Gossip actually help us
reflect on our own lives and make our lives better? Well,

there is a phrase in that movie I really enjoy. It's ***If you don't have anything nice to say about anybody, come sit by me*** " from Olympia Dukakis. It's a funny phrase, and it makes me laugh every time Dukakis says this but there is some true meaning behind this. It really tells us about gossip. How gossip can sometimes help us, can sometimes hurt us and even separate us from those that we love. It's a hard thing to think about what gossip really entails. To get a better look at it, let's take a good look at an example:

"Well, I'll tell ya. (Puts hand on hip, chews gum) Just the other day, I was outside, getting my mail, and I see my neighbor. You know her don't you? Her father used to own the cotton mill down Mill Creek? She's kind of elderly now, and hides in her house, don't ya know on account of her chronic pains in her back, so she says... Anyways, I said, "Hey, Shirley! How ya doin'?" And she comes over, and says, "Oh Hi! Hey, did you hear about Gloria?" and I said, "No, what happened?" Well.....! Shirley starts going off on this really, really lonnnnnng story about how Gloria and her husband are getting a divorce, because she caught her husband cheating, don't ya know. Course, if you knew Gloria, you could hardly blame him for doing that! Yikes! Gag! WOOF! Sooo ANYWAAAAAY.... she says she kicked her husband out of the house, ya know? And she's trying to get rid of all his stuff, and she got a restraining order against him, and....Oh, I'm sorry, were you busy? Is this a bad time? I'm hope I'm not interrupting you."

This was just an example of what Gossip sort of sounds like. There are a lot more details that I left out, but I don't want those Gossipin' ladies in my home town getting mad at me when this book goes viral! It's more like "You hear a juicy tidbit from a friend, who heard it from another friend, who heard it from a person in the hall, who read it on a note passed in math class, which was written by somebody who made it up to get her man jealous."

Anyway, you sort of get my drift about the gossiping that goes around. Now, like I said in the above paragraph, gossip can help, can hurt and can destroy friendships/relationships. So here's the big question: How can Gossiping help us in life?

Great question.

I kind of see gossip as a helping tool. It kind of helps you predict who is friend and who is foe. Even though gossip sometimes isn't all it's cracked up to be, it helps you make up your mind about a person. And who here doesn't want to hear all the juicy tales about the new girl/guy in town? It doesn't just influence your opinions about the people it also influences how you see them. Much does have to do with our need to make sense of what's happening around us. It's human nature to want to know what's happening around us and if the information has a few gaps we try to complete them the best we can. Look how much Facebook and Twitter has helped Gossip in so many ways. You can hear about anything in just a few seconds!! You feel that special belonging in the world. Now you know everything, or close to everything and that's all that matters.

It's also very hard to keep all those feelings bundled up inside of you. We all need a release once in a while and the best way to do that is talk. There is nothing wrong with talking it out with others and it's always great to "listen" to others as well. I believe that's the whole point of the quote: *If you don't have anything nice to say about anybody, come sit by me.* We all have secrets, we all have gossip that we want to share, and we are just waiting on those ears to fill. Will you be the one that is sharing the gossip, or the one listening?

Go forth and re-watch this movie. Which quote do YOU think can help you? And how will this quote help you?

*"If you don't have anything nice to say about anybody, come sit by me."* –Olympia Dukakis in *Steel Magnolias*.

# *November 25, 5:01pm*

# *Day 25*

You don't know me. You've never heard of me before. I'm not somebody famous; I'm not a daughter of a celebrity. The only way you know me is by looking at the last flap of this book and see my smiling face and a little bio of myself on it. You're halfway through this book and you already forgot my name. I don't blame you…you see an interesting title and you want to know who is living through Motion Pictures. Names aren't important. So you have stuck with me for this long and even though you don't know who I am personally or what my name is you have deduced that I love movies. God how I love movies!!!

I have used quote after quote from famous movies and have applied them to my life and I have even shown you how you can apply them to yours as well. After a while you are able to sit down, think of your life and a movie and how you can use your favorite quote from it and make your life totally better.

Now you understand how my life, Miss Kelsey Mecher, enjoys movies and the reason thereof. And not just the My Generation movies, the NOW movies, but also the Classic movies. And when I say Classic I don't mean movies that came out in the '90s. No, I mean the Turner Classic Movies, the movies that show Chaplin, Cary Grant, Fred Astaire, Gene Kelley, June Allyson, and Judy Garland. The Greatest Actors/Actresses of our time and I have seen them all, or most of them!

Thanks to my Mom who immersed herself in old Classic movies and passed that enjoyment down to me did I realize how much movies impact people's lives and how much of a role they play. And I truly believe that if my Mom was like any other parent during my generation's time frame and just liked the chick flicks of the '90s or 2000s, or the horror flicks of this time, I would never have had the pleasure of 'dancing cheek to cheek' or know how much 'going to the St. Louis fair' can mean to a young lady dancing the 'hoochie-coochie'.

I am young, in the mid 20's and I know all there is

to know about Old Classic Movies. Kids are in school talking about Robert Downy Jr., Zac Efron, Jennifer Lawrence, Melissa McCarthy, Idris Elba, and Paul Walker, and here I am talking about Lauren Bacall, Humphrey Bogart, Cary Grant, and Ginger Rogers!!

It amazes me how much people in MY generation have no idea who I am talking about or what movies I am watching while all the time it seems it's vice versa; they tell me about a new movie that came out and I have no idea who the main actors/actresses are because they weren't born in the late 1920s!!! It's so comical at times. Especially where I work.

I work at a library, I believe I stated that before, but to reassure everyone, yes, I am a book geek (not nerd) so I am a Librarian. Many of my co-workers are a little older than I am so I thought here is my chance to see which older movies they watch.

I gotta tell ya….it's like High School all over again!! I mentioned an all-around Old Classic Movie that I was sure they have seen at least once but every SINGLE one of them never saw it! I gotta tell you, it was a little depressing.

An American Classic movie and they never seen it. Oh, of course they have heard of this movie for it is a Classic but have never fully seen it. Plus many quotes from this movie are in movies today. You see a movie or TV Show that has a movie buff character in it who quotes one of the main quotes from this particular movie and everyone is like "Ha-Ha he just quoted from a great movie….never saw the movie but he quoted from it!!"

Every time I asked my co-workers if they have seen this movie, I believe my mouth hit the floor with a very loud THUD! I couldn't believe that they have never seen the classic *"World War II romantic soul-satisfying experience"* ever created!!!!

I have the Two-Disc special DVD of this movie and I placed it in the back room at work and I had everybody take turns watching this movie! I couldn't work in a place where they have never seen Bogey at his greatest!!!!

If you haven't figured out yet what the movie is, then you must be part of the generation that hasn't seen it yet. If you did see it, Bless You! The Classic, Romantic movie of 1942 that touched millions of lives is the one movie that made the song *As Time Goes By* such a heart-stopping love song sung at wedding.

This movie is responsible for the ***We'll always have Paris*** that has made every woman cry and beg their man to take them to Paris; where ***Here's looking at you Kid*** became the best line for men to say at a local bar; where a broken-hearted man can look at the one woman who crushed him all those years ago and say over a bottle of Scotch ***Of all the gin joints, in all the towns, in all the world, she walks into mine*** which in most movies or TV shows that is the most heart-quenching quote a man could ever say to the leading lady!
And who could ever forget the line ***I think this is the beginning of a beautiful friendship*** that has been used over and over in so many different languages!  Yes folks, the movie in question today is none other than ***Casablanca*** starring Humphrey Bogart and Ingrid Bergman.

Many who are reading this will scratch their heads like "I've seen Casablanca, what is she talking about?" Think hard before you say that.  Did you really watch Ugarte get gunned down in Rick's Café Americain after delivering the Papers?  Or see Captain Louis Renault give the order to ***Round up the usual suspects***?  Most of you it's the later, congrats if you really did watch it, I think I'm going to cry for joy if you did!!!

So think very hard….Have YOU seen ALL the WAY THROUGH, the movie ***Casablanca***?  If not, go to your local store and rent ***Casablanca***.  It will change you.  It will transform you.  It will….aw heck. watch it and decide for yourself.

I can tell you though, it really got to me, as all movies apparently do, but this one was different.  This one has two leading characters in love with each other but because of war and destruction they can't see a happy ending for themselves.  They just can't imagine a world where they could live happily ever after with death lingering at their door.  One has seen that so much of his life has gone by and it was all just work and no play until an angel came by and was finally able to let his heart be discovered, while the other has seen so much destruction in her short life that when she found happiness she didn't want to let it go even with the world crashing down upon her, but irrevocably it does.  When that happens how are you supposed to have a happily ever after? But is anything ever a happily ever after?

I'm not going to dwell too much on each and every quote out of this movie although I would love too, but instead try to get you to watch some Classic movies and see how much has changed in the movie industry. And a whole lot of that has to do with the audience and what they want to see.

I'm all for the whole New Generation of movies where there are action scenes upon action scenes. Towns blowing up from a bomb, gun fights blasting everywhere, men fighting for what are rightfully theirs and maybe some storyline is thrown into the midst of things but really gets buried underneath with everything but the telephone poles dressed up in bikinis.

Audiences love those kinds of movies, but they miss out so much on a good storyline. A very well-known actor once said: "You know, I think if you live your life like you're in a movie it will usually inform you of what you do, believe it or not. People are always talking about movies as being make-believe. But the truth is movies construct moments where you get to

watch the screen and decide what kind of man you are."
And that is true. People will watch a character go
through some trials on the screen and the viewer will
look at themselves and see if they could do as such.
As I am re-reading over my picks of books, I start to
realize how much impact movies have had on my life.
How much through the tough times, through the good
times movies were always a part of my life. Whether I
was with my parents, my birth-father, or now by myself
there is always a movie playing that will impact my life.
It seems strange that my life has been brought up with
movies, while others it was camping, or sightseeing new
worlds. I asked my friends what memories they were
fond of as a child and many would say when they went
camping with their family, or went golfing with their dad,
or even traveling to new places, seeing new things with
their family.

Now my parents are the best parents. We did go
camping. We mini-golfed so that counts! We traveled:
been to Chicago, Virginia, Florida, Ohio, Pennsylvania,
Wisconsin, Maryland and lots of other places, so we did
see a vast majority of different states and cultures.

But when a weekend came up that Dad didn't have to go to work, we all looked forward not the "going out" part, but the "What kind of movie-marathon do we want to watch this weekend?" Many of times it was a ***Die Hard*** marathon, or the ***Fast and Furious*** marathon. We would even have the Tom Hanks marathon, Kevin Costner marathon, or my mother's favorite, the Mark Walberg marathon.

What we would do is go to our local Video Plus store downtown and just rent the movies that particular actor is in and that is our weekend. We would sometimes grab Pizza from our  favorite place The Stony Lake Café store; Large Thin crust Supreme on one side (the Parents side) and Pepperoni and Green Olives on the other (My side),  I'd get my Mountain Dew and their Coke or RC. Mom's Wavy chips with one or two French Onion Dip; I, my Doritos and Dad, his Pretzels.

We would do yard work that Saturday morning and around Lunch time we would start our Actor Marathon. To give you a little taste of what one of our marathons was like, (so you can try it at home if you like) one weekend we chose a Humphrey Bogart marathon.

Now that would include of course ***Casablanca, The African Queen*** (my mom's favorite of Bogey's), ***To Have and Have Not,*** and then to top it off we would watch ***Key Largo***.

We sometimes have more if the price is right. That is our weekend. And I say "is" because we still do it. Not constantly like we used to when I was living with them, but now that I have moved out and am on my own we kind of slowed down but haven't stopped completely.

And this has always been in my life, even when I was little. Usually it was my mother and I during the week and then the whole family was together during the weekends for a movie marathon. During the week after school it was my mother and I and TCM, Turner Classic Movies where we would watch old black and whites, sometimes color movies, and that was our time together. Mom loved it because when she was growing up she saw most of these movies in theater when it first came out and she remembers the time frame, what was going on during that time and how much it affected her. She is the real reason why I am into movies so much. Because she watched them when she was growing up she always made sure I was with her watching those movies again!

Now when I'm with my birth-father, wow do the movies change!!! At home with mom I'm watching the old classic movies, when I'm with him, you better believe I'm watching the towns blowing up and the scenes are covered with bikinis! Oh wait, that's James Bond. He always gets a pass!!! Now with him, I love watching movies with him. We would watch a whole marathon of **Rambo, Terminator** and then serve up a dish of maybe a John Wayne marathon. Now those are some classy movies. But that's for another day.

For now, I wanted to inform you how much movies really meant to my family and how that insight to quotes has impacted my life and hopefully to my future children. And now I hope it becomes a part of your life as well.

*"Of all the gin joints, in all the towns, in all the world, she walks into mine. / I think this is the beginning of a beautiful friendship. / Here's looking at you kid. /We'll always have Paris."* - Humphrey Bogart in *Casablanca*

# *November 26, 10:43am*

## *Day 26*

Woke up this morning actually feeling refreshed. I actually was looking forward to writing another quote, sharing my life that is surrounded by movies, with a pen and a piece of paper. I was so pumped up about it. Then I looked at the calendar....it's a Monday. It's a friggin' Monday.

When I was little I always wondered why people had a problem with Monday. It's just another day in the week, a date on the calendar. What's so wrong with Mondays? Then I started to go to school and I realized what people were talking about. There I was having fun during the weekend, not having to worry about exams, homework, teachers asking me questions day in and day out when all of a sudden, BAM! I'm back to answering those hard questions, getting mountains of paperwork I have to do. And Monday doesn't gently ease you back into the system; no it just slams you right in the face!

Same goes for when I started work. Now working at a Library is total fun, don't get me wrong here, but Monday still doesn't ease you in nicely. You've got people calling every minute asking for things, renewing a book; getting a book; faxing; copying; more phone calls.

So I now understand all those memes where a person is holding a huge cup of coffee stating "Keep Calm and pretend it's not Monday". We enjoy the weekend so much we don't want it to end. How does one continue on a Monday? We all dread it, but we still push on and work even though we don't want to.

Some have coffee; some just put on a happy face and work through the pain; some might add that "something something" in their coffee. Me? I actually think of that song "Come Monday" from Jimmy Buffett. To Buffett, Monday was the day when he could see his wife for he was always gone on the weekends for his tour. But Monday was the day that he could be with the one he loves so Monday was actually his best day. So I guess that is how I get through my day; singing "Come

Monday…It'll be alright" and interestingly enough, my Monday's haven't been that bad.

Which kind of got me thinking…what is MY best day? Buffett's best day was the day that he got to see the woman that he loves after a long tour. Everyone has a best day. Something that they look back to, or a favorite day of the week. A lot of people like to look back in their lives and find out what day was their best day, especially when they are having a crappy day. When you are in that crappy state of mind you want to find an event that means something to you so that you can move forward and know that there are more good days than bad and that you can overcome anything that crosses your path.

Interesting isn't it how good always overpowers the bad. "The light shines in the darkness and the darkness can never extinguish it" John 1:5. In everything that we do in life there will always be darkness lurking around to cover our light, but when we remember that light will always outshine darkness, we can be safe from it. The hard part is trying to remember the good during bad times.

So it kind of helps to remember the good times now, so in the future if I run into any kind of darkness, I will be ready to feel good again.

Good days give you happiness, bad days give you experience and worst days give you a lesson, and sometimes you have to go through the worst to get to the best.

Best day? Worst day? Does this sound a little familiar to anybody? I'm trying to think of a movie reference here...I know there is one, there's gotta be. Everyone loves talking about themselves and they love to share their best experiences, their best day, so there has got to be a movie reference.....got it!! Mad Max! No, wait. I don't think that's right. He mostly had bad days in that movie.

Wait, wait I got it. City Slickers with Billy Crystal, Daniel Stern and Bruno Kirby. A movie about three men from the city who are having a mid-life crisis. They decide to do something neither one has ever done before...drive a herd of cattle from New Mexico to Colorado. Kind of hard for city folks who only have ridden in the back of a taxi cab to grab the reins of a horse and make it go where they want it too.

But these three guys are determined to learn how. And in doing so they not only learn how to ride a horse or say Yee-Ha, they also learn a thing a two about themselves and each other. Remember that scene where they are riding together and they start talking about their **_Best Day_**? Such a wonderful scene about them sharing something of themselves that neither friend new. I won't go into too many details of what their favorite days were, don't want to ruin the surprise if you haven't seen it but I do want to share that what they did there was they opened up to each other like they never had before.

Now these are three friends since childhood who stayed friends for a very long time and only NOW are they sharing about themselves. And interestingly enough it was sharing about their best days, even their worst days, that they were able to grow stronger with each other and with themselves.

I've stated beforehand that there are times where I am talking with someone about this book and they always have a quote for me to try out. When I was sharing about

the ***Best Day*** scene in *City Slickers* I can't tell you how
many people LOVE that scene.  They start sharing
THEIR best days with me.  Even when I was talking to
strangers about the scene between the three men, they
wanted to share their own best days, or best experiences
in some cases.  But when I flat out ask "What is your best
day" many times I would get the blank stare and the "tell
you later" speech of how they can't come up with one at
that moment.

It's hard to know what your best day is.  So many
things that happen in day to day life that could be
considered as your best day but to pick just one.

And Phil was right, you can't pick the day your
children were born.  Even though I do not have children
of my own, I know how special that day could be.

Something that means something to only you.  Others
may not be able to understand why this day is so special
to you, but that doesn't matter.  Your best day will only
have special meanings to you.  Like Mark Twain quoted:
*"The two most important days in your life are the day you
are born and the day you find out why."*  Best thing for
one to do is when asked that question, say whatever pops

in your head at that exact moment because that is probably the correct answer. Not sure how that works, but I just go with it!

My best day? Well it seems for me every day is a tie. For you see I work at the most amazing place. I'm a Librarian. I deal with books, I deal with people I can help and I seem important to those that need help.

I have a family that loves me for me. They are not trying to change me to "fit" in or become just like them or follow their footsteps in jobs or personalities. No, they let me choose what I want to do in my life and encourage me to follow through with it. My quirky geeky self and they enjoy me for me.

Of course there are a lot of things in life that I could count as my best day: taking flying lessons and being able to take a solo flight.......being on a music album with my family.....seeing the Cubs win at Wrigley Field.....taking a flight with my folks to Florida to see my Brother and actually spend a whole week with him, not just a quick weekend.

I guess for this year my, best day has got to be the day when my friend Linda asked me to join her on this little quest of writing for a whole month which sprung this energy of writing in me that I forgot I had. Now I will be able to go forward and make writing my life and it all started on my best day.

Go forth and re-watch this movie. Which quote do YOU think can help you? And how will this quote help you? And who can you share this with?

"**_Best Day_**" – Billy Crystal from *City Slickers*

# *November 27, 3:15pm*

## *Day 27*

Visionist: an artist, or an individual that sees beyond what is visible to the eyes of human beings. They are thinkers, they are the brains of society but also very absurd, "nerds" if you will and occasional misfits – in other words they don't fit well into society. They are people with great dreams and great minds. So what I get from that definition is that these brainiacs sees beyond what the world sees.

For example let's look at those Optical Illusion paintings. You may see it one way while others see it another. Like that picture of the young woman, but if you look at it differently you see an older woman in the SAME picture. In this sense, Visionist can see like that optical illusion pictures in the real world. A person walking by; couples eating in a diner; the Real reason for the choices that young man just made. They see the "real deal" in the world.

Wouldn't you like to have a mind like that? A mind that can define what is going on around them and act quickly before anyone else? Nerds like Geoff Johns, Stan Lee, Martin Luther King Jr, John F. Kennedy... and Butch Cassidy.

These are all people (some characters) that can see the inner message in their lives and the lives around them. It's actually amazing on how some people "see" the world. There are those that will "see" what the world wants them to see, and there are those that will actually look beyond the borders and see a whole new perspective of the world.

The thing about a Visionist is that they read between the lines all the time. They don't trust what they are given; they dig deep to find the true answer, they keep fighting for what they believe in to show the Rest of the world the true meanings of things.

That's also another aspect of being a Visionist; you want to share the things you "see", the things that you read between the lines. Share with family, friends, and strangers on a train, Facebook, Twitter, Tumblr or other sources of social media. They will not be stopped; they won't go quietly in the night. No, they want others to know what they know and they aren't afraid to share it.

This entire day has been spent with my parents trying to figure out how I was going to explain this quote in MY life. This particular quote has been used in many different movies/TV shows and everyone loves hearing it for it reminds them of the original home movie of this quote. Especially who was in it, Paul Newman and Robert Redford, two of the greatest actors of their time!!

The movie of choice is non-other than *Butch Cassidy and the Sundance Kid*. If you were sheltered when you were younger from old classic movies, then you probably got this quote for today from Gibbs in NCIS, the TV show that airs on CBS: ***"Boy, I got vision and the rest of the world is wearing bifocals*****."** Yes folks that quote that Gibbs said to DiNozzo is from an old Classic film said by Paul Newman.

Paul Newman's character Butch Cassidy seems to be a man before his time. He sees beyond what the world sees. His vision is clear, when the rest of the world's vision is blurred, or they see only what they're told, or expected to see.

Example: When two people look at a piece of abstract art, the person "wearing bifocals" sees only the structure and the general perception of the art, the person with the "vision" sees the inner message that the artist was imagining, or he sees the different ideas that the artist was designing.

Now mostly this movie is about the two men who rob banks. Not really something that could change my life or yours, but this quote has always stood out for me. But, I couldn't figure out why. That's why I went to my parents, for if I couldn't see it in myself, I know my parents can see it in me.

(This is the part I don't like to do about myself…..talk about myself!!!) Mostly I don't like to brag about myself…to me it looks like bragging but from parents and other people it's more like "informing" you of what I did with my life.

At this moment I am 23years old and I have already: played softball for 3 years (with a .675 batting average); played soccer for 3 years (was actually put as goalie because I was the only girl not  afraid of the ball) l; learned how to play a guitar and sang with my family at the age of 6 and started to perform in front people at the age of 10(recorded solos on our first CD at 10). Then I wanted to have a horse and instead of just jumping the gun and buying one...I went to horse camp for 2 years and learned the ropes of taking care of one and finally got one (her name was Honeybunch, a Sorrell Missouri Fox Trotter, who sadly has since passed away); wanted to learn on how to fly a plane...got the chance to fly solo on November 11, 2011 in a Cessna 150.

When I was a child, way before I could even write words, I would take a notebook and pen and just scribble for hours and hours. When done, my parents couldn't read what I wrote for there were no words but if asked, I could read it to them for I knew what I was writing! Now I am 22 years old, hopefully know how to spell and understand words, and I am writing my first mystery novel and hopefully will write more!!!

There are so many different things that I could have become....a softball player....a professional singer....a pilot, because I saw I had the potential to do these things and had the parents to guide me and say sure...but you're going to need to work hard while you're going to High School (and while I was a Junior in High School I was also going to College on Dual Enrollment).

I used to joke with my HS Principal who allowed me to get out of school early to take my flying lessons only if I promised NOT to land on the football field!!! I mean, I was literally flying an airplane over my high school every day while my friends were taking exams or having to take tests and I'm flying to the Lighthouse by Lake Michigan and enjoying a wonderful view!!!

But because I had the "vision" of myself as a Pilot I went after that dream. I saw myself playing softball, so I went after it! I was curious on how to play the game and my parents helped me and encouraged me in whatever I wanted to do. That's what a visionist means to me. Someone who sees for themselves what they want in life and in this world and what they are capable of doing and they find a way to make that happen!!

It might take a while, it might cost a little but if they are adamant about trying something then they try it! Most everybody is just seeing today…what is in store for them today, sort of like "living in the moment".

For me, it was sort of like living for the future. I'm thinking I could pilot a plane in the near future let's see if it's right for me and I'd try it. Not just waiting for an opportunity to fall in my lap…but to go out there and grab that opportunity before it's too late!!!

So sometimes it's a good idea to look farther into what is going on in your life. Pay attention to your life. Pay attention to the details in your life to where you're going, where you've been and maybe you'll see what is in store for you by knowing what you can and cannot do.

And that is what, to me, Paul Newman was saying when he quoted *"Boy I got vision and the rest of the world is wearing bifocals."*

Go forth and re-watch this movie. Which quote do YOU think can help you? And how will this quote help you?

*"Boy I got vision and the rest of the world is wearing bifocals."* – Paul Newman in *Butch Cassidy and the Sundance Kid*

# *November 28, 5:05pm*

## *Day 28*

It has been one exhausting month.  Been fun, but just so exhausting!!!  Trying to find quote after quote from great movies and seeing if that quote can and will help my life but yours as well.

Even though there might be a quote that will work great for me, it might not have the same meaning to you.  So it's been great going to different stores and asking what is your favorite movie and which quote do you like from it.  And I gotta tell you some of the things people say just gets to me.

Sometimes it takes me a while to get some movie ideas from them for they are too busy trying to think of what is the best answer.  So I finally said I'm going to say Movie and the first movie that pops into your head, say it and we'll go from there.

That worked out so well and I've got to tell you, some of the movies that they said I either never heard of them or haven't even thought of that movie. It's been great. I was talking to my mother (as always) in line at a grocery store and the cashier was interested in what we were talking about, including some of the people around and one of the men suggested *Rocky*, and I almost slapped myself....of COURSE *Rocky*!!! How could I not have thought of that on my own?

I have always loved the movie *Rocky,* the Italian Stallion played by Sylvester Stallone. Loved the whole story of how an underdog fighter gets the chance of a lifetime to fight someone in the big leagues, and was able to not only get to fight him but to beat him at his own game. Rocky surprised everyone, seeing how an underdog, who had nothing, was nothing and became something great. Rocky said right before the fight to Adrian he's nothing. That's all he ever was.

But this is his chance to *Go the Distance* with Apollo Creed. Rocky has a chance to meet Apollo on his level like no other man has before. Apollo has everything, and Rocky just wants to be like that, be able to make a name for himself. In boxing "The Distance" refers to the full number of rounds in boxing matches.

They want you to be able to finish the fight but when there are two fighters that are very good and just keep going, there has to be a limit amount of rounds. And usually it's about 12-15 rounds….like in Baseball there are 9 innings, football there are 4 quarters that last about 15 minutes each and so on and so on.

When a boxer says that he is "going the distance" then that means that that boxer is going for the full 12 rounds without being knocked out. And Rocky tells Mickey that he is ready to Go the Distance with Apollo Creed. He is ready for a fight to remember and not let Apollo's rep knock him down. Rocky also pointed out that he doesn't care if he loses; at least he was able to have the opportunity to fight with a great fighter like Apollo for one night.

And to me in my perspective that is his Distance in Life. That's how far Rocky wanted to go…to be able to have a name for himself, to be proud of being a boxer. Nothing else matters, as long as this is his time, his prime and Apollo gave him that chance.

And that's why I love this movie, because everyone has had doubts in their lives, of their choices they have made for their life. So many men AND women can relate to this.

And then that's when it hits me. *"Go the Distance"* is the PERFECT quote for this book. Even if you aren't a boxer you are a fighter: a fighter in life. You have to fight for your job, for your money, for your family, for your stability to keep going, charging your batteries so to speak and *Go the Distance* is the perfect quote to say to yourself whenever you get into a bind.

I have talked beforehand about being in a position where you are down on your luck, you're not having a very good day, and there are so many great quotes out there that can help lift you back up. And many of those quotes are found in movies that when you hear that quote, you think of the movie; you are thinking of when that quote was said and you either laugh at the remembrance of the scene or the remembrance of the event taking place while watching that scene. I get that more often than not.

For some people this quote means more to them than any other. Mostly for the men, because men seems to appreciate the movie *Rocky* more than woman. Yes it's a boxing movie, a movie about a man finding love in himself, love with a woman and finding his love again with boxing.

I love this movie because I was surrounded by this movie!! And I totally know exactly what Rocky was talking about….just using the slang term of going the distance with a fighter but also Going the Distance with yourself in your life. Going in one more round when you don't think you can – that's what makes all the difference in your life.

If you believe in something, then go the distance. Give it your all. Go all the way to the end. You've got battles that only YOU can face so who's got the right to stop you? They'll try…believe me "they" will try and knock you down and make sure you NEVER reach your goal. Because they can't means you shouldn't, that's the way "they" see it.

There might be some goal that you have dreamed of doing since you were a kid and someone comes along and tells you no but you don't have to listen to them. You *Go the Distance* and you do what YOU can do.

Life will hit ya and hit ya hard, no mistake in that.

Life isn't fair; remember than when you were a kid? It's the truth, I'll tell ya. And when things get hard, and they will, you have to figure out how you can jump back up from that hit and move forward, to finish the job that you started.

So what's your *Distance*? When you say you want to *Go the Distance*, where are you going? What would you like to accomplish that would mean everything to you where nothing else matters? For myself? Finishing this book and actually getting published!!! And if you are reading this, and you are not my mother or any other family member, than kudos for me....I went the DISTANCE!!!!

Go forth and re-watch this movie. Which quote do YOU think can help you? And how will this quote help you? And don't forget....when you hit that rough spot...say this quote while humming: *Da-da-na....da-da-naaaaa...da-da-na....da-da-naaaaa*!!!!

*"Go the Distance"* –Sylvester Stallone in *Rocky*

# *November 29, 4:03pm*

## *Day 29*

For 28 days here I have been, watching movies, dissecting movies, devouring pizza and drowning in Mountain Dew. I believe any second now doctors will be knocking down my door and charging up those paddles and screaming "CLEAR"!!

Again, I had a little trouble picking out which movie to write about. Let's face it folks, I have tons of movies that I can choose from but which one can benefit my life now? That takes some thinking.

I could just sit down and watch movie after movie in one whole day and enjoy every minute of it, but to actually sit down and discuss how that movie was beneficial to my life and yours as well is tough.

Because it could be helpful in my life, but what about yours? Yes, you. The one who is reading this book for God knows why and for some reason I want to help you.

So I needed help. I turned to a person who has been helping me, guiding me along in my life since I was a baby, and loves movies as much as I do. Ladies and Gentlemen I'd like to bring you back to the storyboard here: My Brother.

As I stated beforehand, my Brother plays a huge role in whom I am today and who I am going to be in the future. Always calling me up, giving me advice on school, work, self-being and yes, even boys. That's my big brother for you, always worried that some boy is going to whisk me away and take advantage of my heart and soul and hide me from everyone, never to be seen again!!!
Of course, this is HIS nightmare, not mine. He's just afraid of losing his sister. I keep reminding him he wouldn't really be losing a sister, but gaining a brother...in-law. Of course he never sees it that way!! I remember when I was little; I wanted to be just like him. I would try and get the same big chunky watch he always wore, try to watch the same movies he did, but then that stopped when Mom found out, Ha-Ha!!!

Anyway...enough of family updates and on to

more important values like eating more pizza while trying to find another symbol from a famous movie we humans can use in our day to day lives. And my Brother helped me find one. Well, actually more than one in this case.

As I stated beforehand, Jerry Maguire is one of his favorite movies to watch. And if you remember there was more than one quote that I could have used from that movie. This other movie is a little different. The other "favorite" movie is sort of a Christmas theme that has been used for generations as THE movie to watch during Christmas time. I know it's not just in my family that we keep this tradition going, but probably in yours as well. I know this for a fact…mostly because who in their right mind wouldn't want this movie as their traditional movie for Christmas? Oh, and I asked Google.

And yes, I know it's still November but it's the 29th of November…stores have had Christmas decorations up since before Halloween. Also this movie has very deep meaningful quotes that you don't need to say them just in the winter time….these quotes can be used all season long.

As you can see I said "these" quotes. That is right folks, in this one movie there are at least several quotes that you can apply to your life. I also believe that this is one of the reasons my brother loves this movie…because of all the quotes mentioned in this movie that can apply to anybody's life, but everybody can still interpret differently for these quotes mean something different to everybody.

When I think of Christmas I think of the times I had that year. I know that's generally for New Year's Day, but for me that day is solely for wondering what will come in the next year. What I will be doing, what do I want to do. For for me, Christmas deals with what happened in the past year that I am proud of, that I would love to re-do, or little dilemmas that need to be fixed before next year. And EVERYBODY has dilemmas that they want to resolve for the new year. We all have been working out solutions to little dilemmas once we think of them ever since Charles Dickens wrote that Christmas Carol story of how a greedy man who hates Christmas will get a Christmas present he will never forget: a ghost showing him his past, his present and his future all in one night that would make any man turn for the good.

Every single person who read or saw that story has always wanted that opportunity to see what their life has meant over the years and what the years to come will bring for them.

To be able to see their lives from another perspective always seems to be very fulfilling. But we hardly ever get this kind of chance, so we as have to try and get on with our lives thinking we are doing the right thing. We have to see for ourselves our past that made us who we are in the present, to be welcomed in the future.

Many times, it helps if we have other people standing there telling us, showing us what we are doing with our lives and showcasing for us that we are doing the right or the wrong thing.

Then we are able to move on with our lives, with the help of others. But what if we see our past as a punishment? Then we would not enjoy our present and wouldn't want to see the future. Those kind of people are the kind of people that try hard in life, but things (government, mean people, themselves) put them down, try to discourage them from actually making it in the world and you will believe it all.

You will then start hating your life, and wishing you were never born. Thinking that your town, your society would be better off if you just had not been born.

To be honest, I have felt like this on occasion. When things I needed to get done weren't done on time, or people just discourage me from doing anything good for others or for myself, I start to get down on myself.

Don't lie, you've been here before. Most everybody has been here before. Many suicide cases, this is the answer to why many of them go through with it, mostly because your society keeps putting you down and you are believing the lies.

So you keep thinking, wouldn't life be better if you were never born? What would your family be like? What would your friends be like if you had never entered their lives? Would they be better off? Would they even miss you, even though they had never met you?

Sometimes I wish I had that. Sort of like George Bailey from that small town Bedford Falls. A man who is so selfless, so into helping his community that he never thinks about himself, then when he wants to find happiness for himself, the door keeps shutting hard into his face.

A man who was always there for people, and when it's time for him to need something in return he feels like no one is there for him. He sees his world crashing before his eyes and thinks instead of standing up and asking for help from his own community, he tries to take his own life. But with help from an Angel, Clarence, not Gabriel mind you, he sees that he indeed has been a huge part in making Bedford Falls one of the greatest places to live. And all because of him and his huge heart for the people of the town.

That's right Ladies and Gents....the movie for today that will introduce us to Christmas is none other than *It's A Wonderful Life* starring James Stewart, Donna Read and Henry Travers. The story is about this man, George Bailey, a hysterical, despairing, and melancholy family man who is shown what the small town of Bedford Falls would be like without him.

George is thinking that this little town wouldn't even change if he wasn't around. An Angel 2nd Class named Clarence, comes down to show George Bailey his dream. It's a frightening, nightmarish, view of the world (at Christmas-time) that brings him back from self-destruction.

He sees that not only is he important to this little town, but if he wasn't alive his precious little town would become a different town, destructive and meaningless. When George sees how important his life is, he returns to the idyllic, small-town world that he left, with renewed faith and confidence in life itself.

Hence, the film's title: *It's a Wonderful Life*. Each man's life touches so many other lives. When he isn't around he leaves an awful hole, even if he himself can't see it.

When my brother and I were talking about what kind of quote I could use from such an aspiring movie that would let us really see what life would be like without you, we couldn't decide which quote. So I decided to use all the ones that meant a lot to us and see if they mean anything to you and your life at this precise moment.

Instead of dwelling on each quote, for this day is starting to end, I will give a little tidbit why each quote means so much and you can decide which one suit your life better. I already chose mine, but let's see which one you would choose.

First quote I can remember is "*Just remember this, Mr. Potter that these rabbles you're talking about, they do most of the working and paying and living and dying in this community*." Quick tidbit: George is trying to get Mr. Potter to realize that it's not the money that makes the town...it's the "Rabble" as Mr. Potter likes to call them, and George is trying to tell him and the Board of the Savings and Loan that they are people, actual Human Beings that serve the community and that make the community the way it is. Money doesn't.

"*They'll vote with Potter otherwise*." Another good one about evil, and my Brother pointed out that all that must happen for evil to prevail is for good men to do nothing. Think about that one for a bit, and.... MIND BLOWN!!

There was a part where George is praying in the bar and he states "*Oh God...oh God...dear Father in Heaven I'm not a praying man but if you're up there and you can hear me, show me the way. I'm at the end of my rope, show me the way God*." This one spoke to me a lot. I'm a Christian, and I pray for help or guidance all the time. And for a man who is "at the end of his rope" who does he turn too? To God. Even if you can't pray well, (I mean who can except the Pope right?) anyone can pray to God and He will answer. It might not be the answer you were looking for, but it is an answer. Which then follows up to that line, "*Please God, let me live again*", knowing what kind of life HIS town is leading when he's not there, he realizes how much his life is worth, and how much he himself would miss.

Another of my Brother's favorite is "*ZuZu's Petals*". When he realizes that he is back into his own world, he first realizes that his mouth is bleeding but he didn't fully believe it until he felt those petals from his DAUGHTER'S flower. Mostly this one deals with what exactly ties you down to earth. Everything going on in life, what makes you stop and enjoy your life, the moments of your life? For George it was his daughter's petals.

And of course everybody's favorite, "*Merry Christmas you wonderful, old building and loan*". Even after everything that HE wanted to do in life, after how much that building was the cause for his father's pain and tiredness, he sees what it does for HIS community, so instead of hating it, instead of seeing it as a grave, he sees it as a part of him that means something that nobody else can see. Because of that Building and Loan, his Bedford Falls is what makes it what it is.

My favorite is right there at the end, "*A toast to my big brother, the richest man in town.*" Now Harry doesn't mean all the money that people gave to George, like Mr. Potter would see it. No, Harry means that BECAUSE the town helped out George in time of crisis, BECAUSE it was George the townspeople help him out. You don't see them giving Mr. Potter all that money with a song in their heart.

That's what made George the richest man in town, having that many friends who will help him out in his time of need.

And then another one that I actually almost forgot that follows what I just said. "Remember no man is a failure who has friends." And that is so true. Even if you are poor, living out in the streets, if you have friends, and I mean true friends, how can you be a failure? Being a failure means that you have nothing in life, you let everything in your life down and you have nothing to show for it. But if you can keep a friend, than how is that failing?

I know that is a lot to process and go through, but it's a real meaningful movie when you really think about it.

So go forth and re-watch this movie. Which quote do YOU think can help you? And how will this quote help you?

*"It's a Wonderful Life"* Starring James Stewart and Donna Reed.

# *November 30*

## *Day 30*

Well, folks we have reached the end of our time. It has been a fun, interesting, growing, heartaches-all-around, tear-jerking, and madness time of a month. I don't think I will ever look at November again without pain reaching into my fingers. I swear, I have cracked my fingers more often this month then I ever had in my life time! And I don't believe that a normal person should have consumed that much coffee in 30 years let alone in 30 days!! Oh well, it was worth it! It really was.

I actually have seen myself grow over the past few weeks and I believe I'm a better person inside and out with this challenge. I've met new people (all online of course), learned more about my parents over different quotes, and learned that I can take a movie quote and work it to my advantage and still have a little fun as well.

It was a real learning curve for me. In all the years that I have "started" writing, I never really finished a book, or a short story. I still have piles of notepads in my parent's basement with unfinished stories. And to finish this one; well let me tell you it's a sight for sore eyes. I can scroll up and see the finished work, page after page that I have created not just for myself but for you reader as well. (Hi again, Mom!) Now I can prove to my parents that yes, it might take me awhile to finish something, but this proves that I can finish whatever I started. And from now on I have the confidence in myself that I can finish any project set before me! No fear in these eyes!

But what's so interesting is that it was movies, the life in movies, that changed my life around. As a few quotes ago I mentioned that whenever something was going on in my lifetime, anything bad, sick, or just to keep me occupied, movies were there to sustain me. Watching movies, TV shows kept me afloat through the tough times in my life. But film is not only a model; it is also a mirror and on occasion, a crystal ball. It is easier with hindsight to see traces in films of national concerns and anxieties, signs that might not have been apparent at the time. Over more than 100 years, film has pervaded our sense of ourselves, our ambitions of achievement, even our perception of other countries.

Beforehand. I talked about how this is one deranged child, moi, can know so much about movies, know the quotes by heart. I could have easily been a mushroom. Still time for that I guess. It's about 9:25pm in the evening. Work done with, cleaned the house the best I could for the moment and for most folks, time for bed.

For me, it's time for movies. I can watch movies any time of the day. I could watch one now. What's interesting is that I am sitting here thinking of which movie to watch, and unknowingly, I'm watching all of them...at the same time.

My collections of DVDs are right in front of me waiting for me to select one and play and enjoy it. And here I am just looking at the spine labels of my movies and I can recall almost all the scenes in my head. It is virtually scaring me!!!!!! I'm currently (in my head) watching Frodo and his gang of Hobbits running from the Nasgul and then my eyes shift over to watching Wesley fighting Rodents of unusual size in the forests then jumping to Superman in his new look and new costume fighting Zod and destroying countless buildings one after another.

I can virtually hear Ray Liotta whisper to Kevin Costner "If you build it, he will come". Tom Hanks screaming "Hooooooooch" in that unmistakable voice of his while also hearing him say "Would you like a box of chocolates?" I guess I have turned into a Mushroom.

I have absorbed so much of these movies that my head is practically buzzing with all these scenes, these famous quotes circling around and around in my head. This is my reason for writing this book. If I don't share these quotes, and what they mean to me, I sincerely believe that my head will utterly explode and scripts from famous movies will be pouring out of my head!!!!!
But I'm not complaining. Seriously I'm not. I'm just sharing what is really going on in my head. Maybe you don't really care, but I have to reach my 50,000 words limit and this seemed to help. Ha-Ha!!!!
But this writing down what I'm feeling at this moment with all these movies in my head actually helps me think

clearly. For it's out of my head and onto a piece of paper where if I need to remember I can look it up instead of searching my filled mind for the information. It sort of copies and pastes the information for me so my folders can have more room for more important things to know or remember. I should be able to choose a movie and enjoy it without thinking of my other movies.

Some would say that this girl has no life, and you would be right. But then you would also be wrong for I have lived over a thousand lives already. I love invading books, for there I have lived countless of lives through the characters of those books. I have watched so many movies since I was born that I feel I have been all those characters in all those situations.

For someone that lives in a small town where nothing happens I have lived a wondrous life!!!!! All while sitting in my living room with my closest friends or family. It is such a joy to watch a movie with my parents. For afterwards we always talk about the movie. I believe I stated this before, but for a refresher course, my parents and I will watch a movie, and whatever that movie was, we will sit and discuss about what we thought of it.  What our favorite parts were, why they were the best, and what does this movie mean.

That ladies and gentlemen is where my love of movies began.  The talking with loved ones about something that was so entertaining, so riveting that we get to share what we loved about it and the other person doesn't make fun of your comments, doesn't make you feel like a child with your answers, for everyone sees a movie differently.  So how can one dispute your answers?

Amazing how that one little box with a screen on it can change a life, can make someone's life that is a living hell be a wondrous fantasy.  How that little disc or box (VHS) can make one's life go upside down or put a smile on its broken face.

I guess what I'm trying to say here is....to all the Actors and Actress from all over the world, from all ages....Thanks for the Memories.  Thanks for being there to cheer me up.  Thanks for bringing a smile to my face when the world stole it away.  Thanks for taking me with you to Gotham City, to the Heavenly fields of Iowa, to the streets of Chicago showing us what fun we can have.

Thank you for sprinkling Fairy Dust on us and showing us that we can fly. Thank you for handing us three beans to make our life more adventurous than we could possibly imagine.

And Thank you for fighting our battles for us when no one else would. Thank you so much Hollywood. We owe you a debt of gratitude. Hope this book can cover most of the tab. Enjoy your movies. Enjoy your lives. Enjoy your own happiness. Don't forget to share them with family and friends.

The song by Bob Hope has been always great to hear, to sing in the shower, but it is also a great quote to live by....for me it's the memory that the movies gave me. I remember the old movies, the modern movies and the recent movies. They give me memories that I will cherish for years to come and one day share them with my children.

"***Thanks for the Memories***" – Bob Hope in *The Big Broadcast of 1938*

## ABOUT THE AUTHOR

My Life in Motion Pictures is author Kelsey Mecher-Wentzloff's first book. Kelsey began creating stories even before she could read. Born in Virginia and raised in Michigan, Kelsey has achieved some interesting milestones in her life. An accomplished equestrian, she also soloed in a Cessna 150 airplane; sang and played guitar in a Gospel Band; found her dream job as a Librarian and currently is a Book Reviewer for several publishing companies. A devoted Chicago Cubs and Washington Redskins fan, she enjoys long, romantic walks through bookstores and spends quality time target shooting and watching movies with family.

www.ingramcontent.com/pod-product-compliance
Lightning Source LLC
Chambersburg PA
CBHW051634170526
45167CB00001B/186